Mahatma Gandhi

A man of Peace & Harmony

Mahatma Gandhi

A man of Peace & Harmony

By

Dr. Salahuddin Akhtar Siddiqui

Former Justice, High Court of Nepal
Founder: The Mother Foundation

ADROIT

Adroit Publishers

NEW DELHI • KATHMANDU

ISBN : 978-81-87393-77-1

2020

Published by
ADROIT PUBLISHERS 4675/21, Ganpati Bhawan, Ansari Road,
Daryaganj, New Delhi-110 002 Phone : 011-23266030
adroitpublishers@gmail.com

Typeset in Adobe Caslon Pro by Arun Sharma,
Akriti Graphic Solution, Delhi-110081
E-mail: arun263923@gmail.com, Ph: 9999414390

Contents

Reciting verses in daily morning prayer at Gandhi Ashram

नत्त्वहं कायमें राज्यं नस्वर्ग न पनुभर्वम्।
कामये दु:खतप्रानां प्राणिनामार्तनाशनम्।।

मलाई राज्य को लालसा छैन मलाई स्वर्ग पनि चाहिदैन
मलाई पुनर्जन्म पनि चाहिदैन मेरो एक मात्र इच्छा छ
समस्त दु:खी र संतप्रहरूको कष्टबाट मुक्ति मिलोस

Don't need state power, not heaven, neither needed rebirth, But desire one thing that affected and sad people should get shelter

Bhajan of Mahatma Gandhi

Raghupati Raghav Raja Ram
Patit Pawan Sita Ram
Ishwar Allah tero Nam
Sabko Sammati De Bhagwan

रघुपति राघव राजा राम
पतित पावन सीता राम
ईश्वर अल्लाह तेरे नाम
सबको सन्मति दे भगवान

First they ignore you,
then they laugh at you,
then they fight you,
then you win.

Mahatma Gandhi

Mohandas Karamchand Gandhi's thoughts, values & Teachings

Basic thought

Gandhian philosophy is stay i.e. truth and ahimsa i.e. nonviolence. The other allied thoughts are peace, Satyagrah etc which are born from basic thoughts.

Principle of Gandhian philosophy:

It may be stated as follows: All social action should be governed by the same simple set of moral values, of which the main elements are selflessness, non-attachment, nonviolence and active service.

Basic principles of Gandhi's political thought and the relevance:

Principles for the effective management of political systems in the contemporary world are Truth, non-violence, service and Swaraj. These are the pillars on which Gandhi built his political edifice.

Eternal value:

The ideals of non-violence, freedom, equality and religious tolerance have eternal value of Gandhi ji. He taught us the value of harmonious co-existence and mutual respect.

Truth, non-violence, service, corporate social responsibility, long-term sustainability, excellence are the values of Mahatma Gandhi.

Teaching

Work hard with truth and perseverance to achieve your goal, as a nation and individual self.

Believe in a nation based on equality, free of any disparate based on religion or cast.

Mahatma Gandhi's five values to remember

Self-belief

Believe in what you do and never change your mind even if no one stands by you.

Integrity

Integrity comes from congruence of thoughts, feelings, words, and actions-when all that you are and do spring from your core values.

Respect for all

It is necessary to understand that everybody is equal and they all deserve respect. Money isn't the only factor that gets you respect. Each individual commands respect and it is only fair to give it to them. Always remember the equality for all.

Leadership

- He was by far one of the strongest and most powerful leaders the country has ever seen. Some qualities that are much needed in today's corporate, social and political environment. A leader with a single vision, clear focus and one who wasn't crazy for power.

Simplicity & Humility

- He won the hearts of citizens and followers with his simplicity. No unnecessary publicity, no glamour, no money play just mutual respect. Inspite of being in a position of power he was humble and kind.

- On second thoughts I think in the generation to come, the Gandhi principles will be more relevant.
- Let holidays not mean only leisure mornings and vacations. Let's teach our kids why these days are important.
- You need your kids to tune in to help them understand who Gandhiji was and why we respect him so much.

Top Ten Quotes of Mahatma Gandhi

1. When I admire the wonders of a sunset or the beauty of the moon, my soul expands in the worship of creator.
2. Prayer is not asking. It is longing the soul; it is daily admission of one's weakness. It is better in prayer to have a heart without words than words without a heart.
3. You must not lose faith in humanity. Humanity is an ocean; if a few drops of the ocean are dirty, the ocean does not become dirty.
4. The weak can never forgive. Forgiveness is the attribute of the strong.
5. First they ignore you, then they laugh at you, then they fight you, then you win.
6. Live as if you were die tomorrow. Learn as if you were to live forever.
7. The best way to find yourself is to lose yourself in the service of others.
8. If patience is worth anything, it must endure to the end of time. And a living faith will last in the midst of the blackest storm.
9. Strength does not come from physical capacity. It comes from an indomitable will.

10. Truth is by nature self-evident. As soon as you remove the cobwebs of ignorance that surround it, it shines clear.

Lokendra Bahadur Chand
Former Prime Minister of Nepal
Madhyapur Thimi, Municipality
Ward No. 1
Bhaktapur Lokanthali

लोकेन्द्र बहादुर चन्द
पूर्वप्रधानमन्त्री
Phone: 015182227/9804435689
Email: vsugar68@gmail.com

Persons like Mahatma Gandhi take birth only once in couple of centuries. He influence can't be restricted within the border of a few countries. He and his philosophy has earned world-wide reverance and world-wide acclamation. It is so because what he said were truth that he found in his experiment with truth.

Well, by his weapon of non-violence he won freedom for India which has inspired Asian and African countries to throw away yoke of foreign rule on their shoulders. How could Nepal and immediate neighbour of India resist it and we had also a democratic system in Nepal too.

As far as I know Gandhiji never visited Nepal and never advised Nepalese people what to do. But his charm was so powerful that people were influenced on their own. Well, his influence in Nepal can't be limited to political sphere only. I am not sure but I think that here the progress in the fled of cottage industries, particularly in hand loom may have something to do with Swadeshi movement of Mahatma Gandhi. As a result, India has her Khadi and we have our Gharbuna.

Here we shouldn't forget Sri Tulsi Mehr, a respected person who lived with Gandhiji for a considerable time. He came to Nepal with a spinning wheel and propagated the importance of Swadeshi among the people here.

I can't help saying a few words here about Gandhiji's actions and ideas in short. His dedication for emmunal harmony, his insistence that only ends but means also should be pure, his thrust on the morality in the field of politic and his faith on unto the last are some of his ideas that are a must for the survival of human kind. We can't brush them aside maintaining that Gandhism is too good to be practiced. The solution of the problems confronting the world are found only in Gandhism philosophy. Gandhiji is becoming more and more relevant by the passing of time. The world should not close it seyes and should work for the implementation of Gandhian philosophy.

Well, I would like to congratulate fromer justice and research Scholar Dr. Salahuddin Aklar Siddiqui for his endeavour to pen a book on Mahatma Gandhi. It would be one more feather on this cap as already he has written some enlighting books. I wish him every success.

Lokendra Bahadur Chand

Madhav Kumar Nepal
Former Prime Minister
Senior Leader,Central Secretariate and
Standing Committee Member of
Nepal Communist Party (NCP)
Member, House of Representatives

माधव कुमार नेपाल
पूर्व प्रधानमन्त्री
वरिष्ठ नेता,केन्द्रीय सचिवालय तथा
स्थायी कमिटी सदस्य,
नेपाल कम्युनिष्ट पार्टी (नेकपा)
सदस्य, प्रतिनिधिसभा

असोज ८, २०७६

महात्मा गान्धी बारे

२० औं शताब्दीमा महात्मा गान्धी सत्य, अहिंसा र सामाजिक एवं जातिय तथा धार्मिक सहिष्णुताको आन्दोलनको ICON हुनुहुन्थ्यो । दक्षिण अफ्रिका देखि विशाल भारत सम्म वहाँको दर्शनले लाखौँ-करोडौ मानिसलाई प्रभावित पार्‍यो । राष्ट्रको स्वाधिनताको आन्दोलनका अभियन्ताहरुमा एउटा विश्वास-अतिरिक्त आत्म विश्वास पैदा गर्‍यो । विश्वको अति शक्तिशाली राष्ट्र संयुक्त अधिराज्य, जसको भू-भागमा सूर्यास्त कहिल्यै हुदैनथ्यो-त्यस्तो राष्ट्रले अवलम्बन गरेको औपनिवेशिक नीतिलाई खुला रुपमा चुनौती दिने व्यक्ति- महात्मा गान्धीको विचार, दर्शन र मान्यताका विविध पक्षलाई समेटेर एकजना विद्वान उच्च अदालत, नेपालका पूर्व न्यायाधिश डा. सलाहुद्दीन अख्तर सिद्धिकीले एउटा पुस्तक प्रकाशित गर्ने जमर्को गर्नु भएको छ । “Mahatma Gandhi- A man of Peace and Harmony” पुस्तकले महात्मा गान्धीको जन्म, बाल्य काल, शिक्षा दीक्षा, भारत र पछि लण्डनको पढाई, दक्षिण अफ्रिकाका गोराहरुले काला जाति प्रति गरेको तीतो र अपमान जनक व्यवहारले वहाँलाई स्वराजको निम्ति जुझ्न अभिप्रेरीत गर्‍यो । खास गरी भारतबाट गएका अप्रबासी भारतीयहरुसँग गरिएको व्यवहारले वहाँलाई क्षुब्ध बनायो । जुन कुराले वहाँलाई आत्म सम्मान एवं समान अधिकारको निम्ति स्वाधिनताको आन्दोलनमा उत्रन उत्प्रेरित गर्‍यो । विश्वको त्यस्तो शक्तिशाली राष्ट्रसँग जुध्न आत्म-विश्वास युक्त सत्याग्रह आन्दोलन (शान्तिपूर्ण आन्दोलन) को अग्रणी योद्धाको रुपमा वहाँ अग्रसर हुनुभयो । जेल, नेल, यातना र प्रताडनाले पनि वहाँलाई आफ्नो स्वाधिनताको लडाईको मार्गबाट विचलित बनाउन सकेन । बरु यसले वहाँमा अतिरिक्त बल पैदा गर्‍यो र यो लडाई सम्पूर्ण भारतमा दावानल झैं फैलिन पुग्यो । गान्धीको अहिंस्रक आन्दोलन अगाडी बढ्दै जादा लाखौँ-करोडौं मानिसहरु Quit India Movement (भारत छोड) आन्दोलनमा होमिए । अनि अन्त्यमा ब्रिटिस शासकहरु झुक्न र भारत छोड्न बाध्य भए ।

लाखौं-करोडौ मानिसलाई आफ्नो पछि पछि लाग्न अभिप्रेरित गर्ने व्यक्ति महात्मा गान्धीमा पदीय आकांक्षा कहिले देखिएन । वहाँले राजनीतिमा ब्याप्त पद, सुख र सुविधाको निम्ति मरिहत्ते गर्ने प्रबृतिका बिरुद्ध आजीवन सादा जीवन बिताउने र सामान्य झुपडीमा बास बस्ने वहाँको जीवनशैली थियो । महात्मा गान्धीमा अतिरिक्त आंट र आत्म बिश्वास रहेको पाइन्छ ।
सत्य र स्वराजको निम्ति अहिंसा र सत्याग्रहको बाटोबाट जीत हुन्छ भन्ने एउटां अचम्मको आत्म विश्वास महात्मा गान्धीमा थियो । वहाँमा स्वतन्त्रता, पारस्परिक सम्मान सद्भावयुक्त सहअस्तित्व, निस्वार्थता, धार्मिक सहिष्णुता र सक्रिय सेवाको मूल्य र मान्यतामा गहिरो विश्वास थियो ।
यसैकारण पनि महात्मा गान्धीत्यस्तो राजनेतामा स्थापित हुनुभयो जो बिरलै पाइन्छन् । गान्धीबाट प्रभावित भएर नेल्सन मण्डेलाले अहिंसा कै माध्यमबाट स्वराज र स्वतन्त्रता प्राप्त गर्न सफल हुनुभयो ।
गान्धीको अहिंसक आन्दोलनको प्रभाव नेपालका कतिपय नेताहरुमा परेको पाइन्छ । नेपालमा शुक्रराज शास्त्री गान्धीको विचार-दर्शनबाट सबै भन्दा पहिला प्रभावित हुनु भयो । महात्मा गान्धीकै विचार र दर्शनबाट प्रभावित भएर तुल्सी मेहर जस्ता व्यक्तिले चर्खा प्रचारक अभियान संचालन गरी स्वदेशी कपडा उत्पादनको अभियान चलाउनु भयो । जन चेतना जगाउन, जनतामा आत्म विश्वास पैदा गरी अधिकार प्राप्तिको निम्ति अघि बढ्न वहाँले युवाहरुलाई उत्प्रेरित गर्नु भयो । संयुक्त राष्ट्रसंघले अक्टोबर २ तारिखलाई अहिंसा दिवसको रुपमा विश्वव्यापी रुपमा मनाउने निर्णय गरेको छ । यस्ता आदर्श पुरुष महात्मा गान्धीप्रति म हार्दिक श्रद्धान्जली र सम्मान व्यक्त गर्न चाहन्छु । वहाँका दुरदृर्शीपूर्ण सोच र दर्शनले आम जनतालाई कर्तव्य पथमा निष्ठा र विश्वासका साथ अघि बढ्न साथै प्रेरणा प्रदान गरिरहोस् ।

माधवकुमार नेपाल

Residence : 503/40022-Fulbari Marg, Koteshwor-35, Kathmandu-44600, Nepal, P.O. Box: 24148, Tel: +977-1-4602303, Fax: +977-1-4600609
Website : www.madhavnepal.com, E-mail : gamknepal@gmail.com **Office :** Dhumbarahi, Kathmandu, Tel : +977-1-4378055, 4378090, Fax : +977-1-4015980

Preface

Keeping in mind the objectives of 'The Mother Foundation Nepal', a non-profit sharing, service oriented institution, to strengthen relation with our friend nations for the peace & development of Nepal, I decided to collect information to write on a spiritual & political leader "Mahatma Gandhi", Father of the Nation of our neighbour India.

A young barrister of middle class family Mohandas Karam Chand Gandhi fought for independence of his country. And by his noble cause with clear vision and action of non-violence a simple man became a 'Mahatma' who is well known as 'Mahatma Gandhi' throughout the world.

Being Mahatma, Mohandas had no craze for the power. He was Hindu by religion having secular thought. As he said- he read many Holy Scriptures including Holy Quran several times and 'Life of Prophet Mohammad (PBH). His ascetic life in simplicity, kindness & love including his respect to all the religions titled him 'Mahatma'. His movements like Satyagrah, non-violence, Sarvodaya etc. reflect the spirit of scriptures. He was Indian so fought for Indians but his massage was International which is still relevant today as it was then.

India is immediate southern neighbour of our country having International boarder open for the citizens of both the countries. Such relation & trust is unique which should be strengthening more in days to come which is necessary for peace & development of both the countries. I hope this book may play catalytic role enhancing trust between each other.

Here I would like pay my sincere gratitude to Former Prime Minister Rt. Hon'ble Mr. Madhav Kumar Nepal & Former Prime Minister Rt. Hon'ble Mr. Lokendra Bahadur Chand for providing his massage for this book and all my other beloved friends including Mahesh Sharma, Librarian of Nepal Bharat Library and Mr. Akhil Sharma, who encouraged me very much writing & publishing this book.

At the last but not the least I also thanks to Board of Directors of The Mother Foundation, Miss Tabassum Siddiqui-President, Dr. Aamir Siddiqui, Er. Mohd. Asif Siddiqui, Miss Tarannum Siddiqui who has assisted me, physically & economically, as they can, completing this book.

Dr. Salahuddin Akhtar Siddiqui
Former Justice

Chapter -1

Child Hood of Mohandas

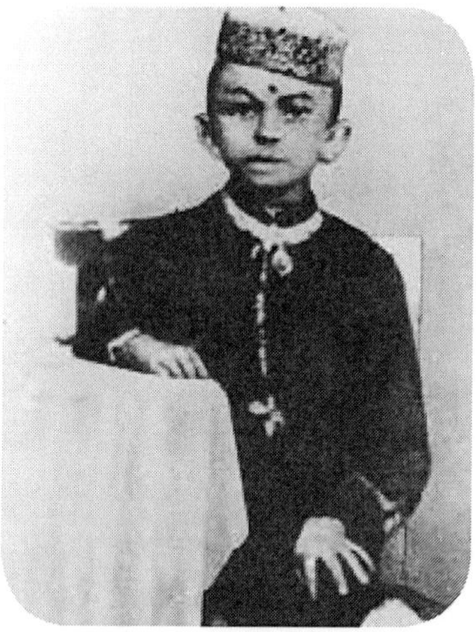

A humble family of merchants in Porbander on the cost of Kathiwada in western India was led by Uttamchand Gandhi, become the Dewan of Porbandar. Porbandar was an old sea-port, overlooked by the distant Barda Hills. Uttamchand Gandhi was succeeded by his son, Karamchand Gandhi popularly known as a Kaba Gandhi. Karamchand had very little formal education, but his knowledge and experience made him a good administrator. He was brave, generous but had short temper. His wife Putlibai was deeply religious and widely respected for her wisdom and good sense. Their family were famous for their ability and their upright character.As a whole it was a eclectic family.

Karamchand Gandhi and Putlibai had borne a small and dark boy, in a small, white-washed house on October 2, 1869 AD, who had no difference from the millions of other children born in India. He was named "Mohandas". Mohandas was the youngest of the six children of Kaba Gandhi. Mohandas was the favourite child of the family and was called 'Moniya' by his fond parents and their friends. Moniya adored his mother but he loved his father too. He was a little afraid of him.

As a child, Moniya seldom liked to stay at home. He would go home for his meals and then run away again to play outside. If one of his brothers teased him or playfully pulled his ears he would run home to complain to his mother. 'Why didn't you hit him? She would ask. How can you teach me to hit people, mother? Why should I hit my brother? Why should I hit anyone? 'Would be Maniya's prompt reply. His mother wondered where her little son got such ideas. Moniya was just seven years old when father left Porbandar to become the Dewan of Rajkot.

❍❍❍

Chapter-2

School days of Mohandas

Mohandas was born at Porbander but at the age of seven years his family moved to Rajkot. At Rajkot, Mohandas was sent to a primary school of all boys. He was shy and did not mix easily with the other children. Every morning he went to school in time, and ran back home as soon as school was over. His books were his sole companions and he spent all his free time alone reading.

He had one friend, however, a boy named Uka. Uka was a sweeper-boy and an untouchable. One day Moniya was given some sweets. He ran at once to Uka to share them with him. 'Don't come near me little master,' said Uka.'Why not?' asked Moniya, greatly surprised. 'Why can't I come near you?' 'I am an untouchable master,' Uka replied. Moniya took hold of Uka's hands and filed them with sweets. His mother saw this from a window, and she ordered Moniya to come in at once. Don't you know that high caste Hindu should never touch an untouchable? She asked sternly. 'But why not, mother?' asked Moniya. 'Because our Hindu custom forbids it,' she said. 'I don't agree with you, mother. I find nothing wrong in touching Uka. He is not different from me, is he? His mother had no answer. She angrily told him to go and have a bath and say his prayers.

Karamchand Gandhi, the father of Mohandass loved all his sons, but he was especially fond of the youngest. He often said to him: 'You must go to high school and college and take up a profession. 'Moniya worked hard, and did his lessons carefully. But he did not learning by heart and was therefore weak in Sanskrit. Geometry he liked best because it involved reasoning.

Once, Moniya happened to read the story of Shravana Kumar. Shravana's parents were old and blind, and he always carried them with him in two baskets slung on a yoke. Moniya was deeply touched by Shravana's devotion to his old parents. At about this time he also saw a play about Harishchandra, a King who was famous for his love of truth. Why shouldn't we all be truthful like "Harishchandra"? He constantly asked himself.

Mohandas was only thirteen years old when he was told to get married with a 14 years old girl of Kapadia family. His parent has already chosen his bride. In May, 1883, the Mohandas married to "Kasturbai Makhanji Kapadia" in shortened to "Kasturba". It was child marriage. Kasturba was a pretty and lively girl. Mohandas and she often played together. Sometimes Mohandas tried to teach his young wife, but she could never concentrate on books, though she was quick to learn the household work.

Recalling the days of their marriage, Gandhi ji once said, "As we did not know about marriage, for us it meant only wearing new cloths, eating sweets and playing with relatives." As was prevailing tradition, the adolescent bride was to spend much time at her parent's house, away from her husband.

One day Mohandas met Sheik Mehtab, a friend of his elder brother. Mohandas was much impressed by Mehtab because he was strong, tall and handsome. Being a Muslim, Sheik Mehtab was a meat-eater. He advised Mohandas that if he ate meat he would also grow tall and strong. At that time it was a reform movement for a change in the orthodox ways of life. Mohandas himself had heard that many well-to-do people had started eating meat. He did not like the taste of meat but as time went on he started to like meat curries. Whenever Mohandas had a meat meal outside, he had to give his a mother some excuse for not eating his dinner. He knew that his parents would not forgive him if they knew he had eaten meat. He was not against eating meat then, but he was against telling a lie to his mother. This feeling was gnawing at his heart and finally he decided not to touch meat again. Mohandas has also taken to smoking with his friends, brother, and another relative.

One day, in order to pay off a debt which his brother had incurred, Mohandas stole a piece of gold. Stealing was a great sin. He knew that he had committed a great crime. He resolved never in his life to steal again. He wrote down a confession of his crime and handed the paper to his ailing father. Karamchand Gandhi read the confession. He tore up the paper without saying a word. The bits of paper fell to the floor. He sank back on his bed with a sigh. Mohandas left the room, tears streaming down his face. From that day, Mohandas loved his father more and more. Every day he hurried home from school to wait on him.

In late 1885, when Mohandas was only sixteen year old his father died. At the age of 16 when his wife was the age of 17 had their first baby, who survived few days only.

In November 1887 at the age of eighteen Mohandas graduated from High school in Ahmadabad. In 1888, he enrolled at "Samadas" college in Bhavnagar but left after one term.

❍ ❍ ❍

Chapter-3

Mohandas as Student of Law

Mohandas was encouraged and advised that he would learn Law studies in London because such types of studies were not available in India, though he was belonged to poor family. In July 1888, his wife Kasturba gave birth to their first surviving son, Harilal. His mother was not comfortable about Mohandas leaving his wife and family, and going so far from home. Mohandas's uncle Tulsidas also tried to dissuade his nephew. Gandhi wanted to go. To persuade his wife and mother, Gandhi made a vow in front of his mother that he would abstain from meat, alcohol and women. Mohandas's brother Laxmidas, who was already a lawyer, cheered Mohandas's London studies plan and offered to support him. Putlibai gave Mohandas her permission and blessing.

On 10 August 1888, Mohandas Gandhi aged 18, left Porbandar for Bombay. Upon arrival, he stayed with the local Modh Bania community while waiting for the ship travel arrangements. His Modh Bania community opposed to go abroad to study because none had did so. Religion was barrio to travel abroad. He intended to go abroad to study. The head of the community knew Gandhi's father. After learning Gandhi's plans, he and other elders warned Gandhi that England would tempt him to compromise his religion, eat and drink in Western ways. Gandhi informed them of his promise to his mother and her blessings. The local chief disregarded it, and excommunicated him from his caste. But Gandhi ignored this, and on 4 September, he sailed from Bombay to London. His brother saw him off.

Gandhi sailed to London on SS Clyde, a ship belonging to the Peninsular & Oriental Company. That company was best and most popular boat and it also carried the royal mail to London. The ship Gandhi travelled on had been built by William Denny & Brother of Dumbarton and was launched on 14, June 1881. She was built to carry 123 first class and 48 second class passengers. Gandhi liked the arrangement of the ship very much. He admired the "dexterity of the workmen and the sailors", and every now and then he himself "played upon the Piano." He was enthusiastic to the deck, where he could get fresh air, and talk to fellow passengers.

Arriving on 29 September 1888 to Britain, Mohandas immediately went to the Victoria Hotel on Northumberland Avenue. Recalling that event later Gandhi ji wrote in his autobiography that living in Hotel was a trying affair and expensive. Northumberland remains hotel until the

Second World War. When the building requisitioned as the Ministry of Defence and renamed Northumberland House. Today, it is a residence for student of the London School of Economics. Gandhi moved to staying with a friend for a month [at Richmond], who treated him kindly and taught him how to behave and how to use the fork & spoon. Then Gandhi moved to a family of an elderly Anglo-Indian widow in West Kensington for a year. Mohandas Gandhi had enrolled at the Inner College Temple in November 1888, as Law student.

At first, for a brief period in 1888-89, Gandhi takes on a difficult task to become an 'English gentleman'. He bought new cloths at the Army and Navey stores. "Wasted 10 pound on an evening suit made in Bond street" and took lesions in dancing, French and elocution". Finding dancing lessons too difficult, he decided to buy a Violin and asking a teacher to help him to play it. However, after three few months, Gandhi gave up these pursuits, declaring that "If my character made a gentlemen out of me, so much me better". Gandhi gave a detailed account of how he managed to live 1888-1889 in his writing "Guide to London".

Since, "the Bar examination did not require much study". Mohandas attended University College, London which is a constituent college of University of London. Besides his law studies Gandhi resolved to pass the London matriculation examination in June 1890. Which would added to his "stock of general knowledge, without any extra expense worth the name" He failed the first time in December 1889 due to his difficulties with Latin, but preserved, and successful in passing the Matriculation examination with Latin, French and paper on Heat and Light instead of Chemistry.

Gandhi as young student came to England to satisfy his "curiosity of what London was." Gandhi used his experiences as a law student in London to write a **Guide to London**, addressed mainly to other Indian who wished to travel to England to study Law.

Gandhi suggested to young Indian students in "A chapter for Would-be Barristers" of Guide to London "Supposing then, that you have made up your mind to become a Barrister, the first thing for you to do is get a certificate of your having passed the matriculation examination. If you have not passed the matriculation examination, you will be required to pass an entrance examination before admission. They examine in History and Latin, but Indian students are by an application exempted from the Latin examination".

Those who have joined some universities are exempted from the payment of 100 Pound in the beginning, though they have to pay the sum in the end to the respective Inns. There are Four Inns, viz., Inner Temple, Middle Temple Lincon's and Gray's Inn. From economic point of view Lincon's Inn was the best. Middle Temple was more patronized by the Indians. From the education point of view, all the Inns are equal because they have a common examination.

One has to keep twelve terms before being call to the bar. There are four terms every year, the first in January, the second in April, the 3rd in June, and 4th in November. The shortest term lasts 20 days and the longest about 31 days.

Keeping term means taking dinners in the respective Inns to which you belong; you have not necessarily to take your dinner but you must go to the dining hall punctually at the appointed time and sit there for one hour. You are said to have kept one term when you have attended six dinners in the term. Those who belong to a university have to attend only three dinners. These dinners, whether partaken of or not, have to paid for. And such dinner have to be taken 12 times.

To be fit for being called to the Bar at the end of 12 terms, two examinations must be passed, one in Roman law and other in the English Law. A student can appear in the Roman law examination after-but not before-keeping four terms. The other examination called the Bar final a student can appear in it after-but not before- keeping nine terms, i.e. at the end of two years after admission. This time, too, is more than enough for the examination. The examination takes place in the law of property, common law including criminal law and Equity, and lasts for four days, but now there are two equity papers instead of one.

A notion seems to prevail in many quarters that students are called to Bar without any examination. No doubt the examinations are easy or, rather, found to be easy.

Students generally study for themselves through lectures common to the four Inns Special lectures, too, organized by each Inn. These lectures are generally attended by those students who want to compete for scholarship.

Call to the Bar is a mere formal ceremony. After you are called, a certificate is given to you and you have to apply for special certificate if you want to practice in India or the colonies. Before leaving England, students, now Barristers, generally get their names enrolled in Her Majesty's High Court of Justice.

During his stay in England Mohandas did not participate in the newly established British Committee of the 'Indian National Congress' but did attend meetings of the 'London Indian Society'. He also attended meetings of the Anjuman-e-Islam (after 1903 called the Pan-Islamic Society), the National Indian Association', and the 'Northbrook Indian Society'.

Before leaving for London, Mohandas had promised his mother not to eat meat. He found it difficult at first but soon discovered vegetarian restaurants and joined the London Vegetarian Society. He often wrote for their journal the Vegetarian and became a member of the Executive Committee on 19 September 1890. Gandhi had also come into contact with the 'Theosophical Society' in 1889, and was introduced to 'Annie Besant' before he left London on 12 June 1891.

At UCL, Gandhi studied law and jurisprudence. In his autobiography, Gandhi was to admit that he succeeded in turning the examination into a difficulty. And he was invited to enrol at 'Inner Temple' with the intention of becoming a barrister. He read Roman law in Latin. Using the knowledge of Latin he had acquired while passing his matriculation examination in London. Gandhi took nine months of "fairly hard labour to read through the Common Law of England. He found Broom's Common law an interesting, but big volume. Snell's Equity, was for him a little bit hard to understand. He took interest in White & Tudor's Leading cases and Goodeve's Personal Property, along with William's and Edward's Real Property.

His childhood shyness and self withdrawal had continued through his teens, and he remained so when he arrived in London, but he joined a public speaking practice group and overcame this handicap to practise law.

His time in London was influenced by the vow he had made to his mother. He tried to adopt "English" customs, including taking dancing lessons. However, he could not appreciate the bland vegetarian food offered by his landlady and was frequently hungry until he found one of London's few vegetarian restaurants. Influenced by Henry Salt's writing, he joined the 'London Vegetarian Society' and was elected to its executive committee under the aegis of its president and benefactor Arnold Hills. An achievement while on the committee was the establishment of a local 'Bayswater chapter'. Some of the vegetarians he met were members of the 'Theosophical Society' which had been founded in 1875 to further universal brotherhood, and which was devoted to the study of Buddhist and Hind literature. They encouraged Gandhi to join them in reading the '*Bhagavad Gita*' both in translation as well as in the original.

He passed his Roman law examination in March 1890 and passed the Bar finals in January 1891. Mohandas Karam chand Gandhi at the age of 22 years was called to the Bar on 10 June 1891.He was enrolled in High Court London on 11 June 1891. On 12 June sailed for Bombay after three years in England. For his voyage, Gandhi took the express train from Liverpool street station in the city of London to catch P&O ship, the SS Oceana. Gandhi reached Bombay on 5th July 1891.

❍❍❍

Chapter-4

Mohandas Karamchand Gandhi as young Barrister

After getting all the certificates and becoming young barrister Gandhi left London for India, where he learned that his mother had died while he was in London and that his family had kept the news from him. Whilst in Bombay he began to study Indian Law. The study of Indian law was a tedious business. The civil code procedure code he could in no way get on with. He developed some linking for the evidence act and read Mayne's Hindu Law with deep interest. At that time he took a case of Mamibai but it was small case. Gandhi appeared in court but could not cross examine the plaintiff's witnesses. He hastened from the court and decided not to take any more case until he had courage enough to handle it. Gandhiji was used to attend High court daily whilst to Bombay; he could not say that he had learnt anything there.

His attempts at establishing a law practice in Bombay was least successful because he was psychologically unable to cross-examine the witnesses. He returned to Rajkot to make a modest living drafting petitions for litigants, but he was forced to stop when he ran afoul of a British officer Sam Sunny.

In 1893, a Muslim merchant in Kathiawar named Dada Abdullah contacted Mohandas. Abdullah owned a large successful shipping business in South Africa. His distant cousin in Johannesburg needed a lawyer, and they preferred someone with Kathiawari heritage. Mohandas Gandhi inquired about his pay for the work. They offered a total salary of £105 plus travel expenses. He accepted it & he set sail for South Africa to be the lawyer for Abdullah's cousin. He spent 21 years in South Africa as young Barrister. He raised his family, established himself as a lawyer.

As Civil rights activist in South Africa

Mohandas Karamchand Gandhi, during his stay in South Africa, worked as Lawyer and side by side he developed himself civil right activist. He also strengthened his political views, ethics and politics.

Immediately upon arriving in South Africa, Gandhi faced discrimination because of his skin colour and heritage, like all people of colour. He was not allowed to sit with European passengers in the stagecoach and told to sit on the floor near the driver, then beaten when he refused; elsewhere he was kicked into a gutter for daring to walk near a house, in another instance thrown off a train at 'Pietermaritzburg' after refusing to leave the first-class. He sat in the train station, shivering all night and pondering if he should return to India or protest for his rights. He chose to protest and was allowed to board the train the next day. In another incident, the magistrate of a 'Durban' court ordered Gandhi to remove his turban, which he refused to do. Indians were not allowed to walk on public footpaths in South Africa. Gandhi was kicked by a police officer out of the footpath onto the street without warning.

When Gandhi arrived in South Africa, according to Herman, he thought of himself as "a Briton first, and an Indian second". However, the prejudice against him and his fellow Indians from British people that Gandhi experienced and observed deeply bothered him. He found it humiliating, struggling to understand how some people can feel honour or superiority or pleasure in such inhumane practices. Gandhi began to question his people's standing in the British Empire.

The Abdullah case that had brought him to South Africa concluded in May 1894, and the Indian community organised a farewell party for Gandhi as he prepared to return to India. However, a new Natal government discriminatory proposal led to Gandhi extending his original period of stay in South Africa. He planned to assist Indians in opposing a bill to deny them the right to vote, a right then proposed to be an exclusive European right. He asked 'Joseph Chamberlain', the British Colonial Secretary, to reconsider his position on this bill. Though unable to halt the bill's passage, his campaign was successful in drawing attention to the grievances of Indians in South Africa. He helped found the 'Natal Indian Congress' in 1894, and through this organisation, he moulded the Indian community of South Africa into a unified political force. In January 1897, when Gandhi landed in Durban, a mob of white settlers attacked him and he escaped only through the efforts of the wife of the police superintendent. However, he refused to press charges against any member of the mob.

By 1906, he had emerged as the spokesman of Indians in Natal and Transvaal and in October that year he was once again in London to speak on behalf of the Indian community. In London he met with Lord Elgin to discuss the rights of Indians in South Africa, but upon his return in December 1906, Gandhi was disappointed. Imperial politics brought Gandhi to London again in July 1909. However, what concerned Gandhi the most this time was the status of highly educated Indians. In August, he visited Louth with his friend Pranjivan Mehta; later in August he visited George Allen in the Cotswolds, and on 7 November he spoke to the Indian students at Cambridge. On his voyage back to South Africa, he wrote his powerful book Hind Swaraj, or Indian Home Rule, in which he wrote about his increasing discontent with the West, the power of non-violence and the vision of self-rule.

Between 1909 and 1914, Gandhi received several invitations to return to India, but before doing so he visited London again in August 1914, two days after the outbreak of the First World War. The purpose of his trip was to visit his friend and mentor G. K. Gokhale but he had already left for Paris. With Gokhale gone, Gandhi met the poetess Sarojini Naidu instead. On 8 August, a reception was held for him at the Hotel Cecil. In attendance were, among others, Charlotte Despard, Albert Cartwright, Bhupendranath Basu, Sacchidanand Sinha, Lala Lajpat Rai, Mohammed Ali Jinnah, Ananda K. Coomaraswamy, Amir Ali and J. M. Parikh. While in London he established the Indian Volunteer Corps before he left on 19 December 1914.

From 1919 Gandhi became highly politically active in India. It was his belief in satyagraha that made him the leader of the nationalist movement against the Raj. By 1931 he had become integral to Indian national life and the sole representative of the Indian National Congress at the second Round Table Conference (Gandhi was in prison during the first Conference in 1930). He arrived in September 1931 and gave his first speech at the Conference on 15 September. The Second Round Table Conference failed to yield independence for India, and Gandhi left London on 5 December 1931. Back in India Gandhi continued to promote satyagraha and led the Quit India Movement in 1942. On 30 January 1948, Gandhi was walking through the grounds of Birla House, New Delhi, when he was shot at point blank range by Nathuram Godse.

Chapter-5

Religion and Gandhi

What is Religion?

The word "Religion" which was comes from word "*Religare*" means 'to tie, to bind fast'. The etymology is favoured by many based on its ability to explain the power religion has over people and communities in which they live. Religion is commonly, but not always, associated with a particular system of faith and worship of a transcendent deity or deities. It derived from Latin *'Relgio'*, respect for what is sacred, reverence for God. Religion is cultural system of behaviour and practices, world view sacred texts, holy place, ethics.

Simply Religion is defined as-

- The belief in a God or a Groups of God
- An organized system of belief, ceremonies and rules used to worship a God or groups of Gods.

Types of religion;

There are three categories of religion:

1. Religion, a term which refers to trans-cultural faith
2. Indigenous religion, which refers to a smaller, cultural- specific or non specific religious group.
3. New religious movement, which refers to recently developed faith.

In Human rights discourse, however, the use of the term "Religion" also includes support for the rights to non-religious beliefs, such as 'Atheism' or Agnosticism. In 1993, the human rights committee, an independent body of 18 experts selected through UN process, described the religion or belief as-'theistic, non-theistic belief, as well as the right not to profess my religion or belief'.

Religious and non-religious belief brings hope and consolation to billions of people across the globe, and hold great potential for peace and reconciliation. They have also, however, been the source of great tension and conflict. This complexity and the difficulty of defining "Religion and Belief" inclusively, is illustrated by continuing struggle to protect freedom of religion or belief in context of International Human Rights.

Gandhi & Religion:

Gandhi was primarily a man of religion. His religion was based on truth and love, and non-violence. It is his religion that became his philosophy of life, and it gave him strength. Gandhi expressed the opinion that religion can become a basis for friendship among all mankind. He strongly believed that religion does not teach mutual enmity.

Discussing with the representative of "Times of India" on November 21, 1932, Gandhi clarified that "I am both an Iconoclast and an Idolater. It is a very different thing from saying that I have no faith in image worship? But if someone says that I hardly ever go to temple, it will be quite true. I would not like to go into the reason why I don't visit the temple. But I will say this: that my religion is so all-embracing that I go with the same devotion to a Hindu temple, a Muslim Mosque, a Christian Church or a Jewish synagogue. I have never gone to any of these places as an atheist or a critic, but always with full devotion." (Mahadevbhaini Dairy,vol.II,pp.261-2).

He considered that different religions as the different roads going towards the same destination. Gandhi out of his own experiences and readings came to the conclusion that all religions are based on the same principles, namely, truth and love. He claimed that religion is a binding force and not a dividing force. He was greatly perturbed by the fighting among people in the name of religion, and, in fact, laid his life for the sake of religious unity.

Gandhi believed in the concept of 'Sarvadharma Samanatva', which means equal respect for all creeds and faiths. But he very clearly stated that equal regard does not mean that one should adopt other's religion. It only refers to understanding the opinions expressed by other religions while adhering to one's own views.

It means emphasizing on the point of agreements than on disagreements. By being a Hindu, Gandhi considered religion as being most tolerant and that it gives scope for worshiping all prophets of the world. Gandhi once quoted that Hinduism tells everyone to worship God according to his/her faith or dharma, and hence it lives at peace with all other religions. Hinduism, according to Gandhi, is not a mere religion, but a way of life, wherein there is a relentless pursuit of truth. Gandhi was successful in understanding the spirit of other religions, especially by virtue of being a Hindu.

According to Gandhi, the main aim of religion is to make a one-on-one interaction between God and humans. He believed God is identical with truth. He perceived God through the service of humanity, because God lives in the heart of every human being or for that matter in every one of his creations.

Gandhi believed that there is no issue of having only one religion because God himself created different religions and no one has the power to question the same. Gandhi opined the ultimate aim of the human being is the vision of God and for this purpose, all activities—be it social, political or economic—must aim at the realization of God.

Gandhi supported two different notions of reality that helped in correctly judging the faiths of various religions. He had a balanced regional approach that led him to take the whole world in the embrace of his love. He believed in the twin doctrine of 'Satya' and 'Ahimsa'. The term 'Satya' means truth and 'Ahimsa' means non-violence.

These two principles helped Gandhi in evolving a comprehensive view of religion that was far beyond the narrow sectarianism. For Gandhi there is no higher way of worshipping God than serving the poor and identifying God in them.

He, out of personal choice, wanted to travel in third class compartment and usually clad himself in a loin cloth that reminded him that he was one among the poor millions and that he belonged to the lower order of mankind and where humanity and love were found to be the richest.

Gandhi understood the term 'love' in terms of non-violence. It was based on this understanding that Gandhi attempted to enlighten people that differences in the various religions were only in terms of their approach to God. He believed that truth and love are the two instruments that bind us to one another and also to the God.

Gandhi further laid out three important virtues of a religious person: firstly, truth as a divine quality, secondly, non-violence or ahimsa and thirdly the virtue is 'Brahmacharya'. He opined that ahimsa as the supreme religious duty in accordance with the teachings of the Mahabharata. If one does not believe in non-violence, he has no kindness for others. Thus, sympathy and kindness towards all men becomes the basis of true religion.

In simple terms, religion for Gandhi consists of worshipping God or reading a religious book. Religious life meant identification with mankind. He regarded religion as self- realization, as the striving of the human personality to express itself in service, suffering and sacrifice.

Further, Gandhi had a very rational outlook towards religion. He opined that religion should be able to solve the day-to-day problems because it is a practical discipline. He out-rightly rejected any religion that does not appeal to reason and is in conflict with morality. He believed that once humans lose their morality they cease to be religious, and selfishness and narrow-mindedness creep in.

Thus, religion demands genuine consideration for all faiths. Through his prayer meetings, Gandhi tried to give a broad basis for religious outlook of man. This is, in fact, the greatest contribution of Gandhi towards religion and thereby the ideal of universal brotherhood. However, during his last years, he was greatly disturbed by the communal tensions in the country.

In one of the prayer session messages, he stated that if love could not affect people, then it would be best God takes him away. This statement suggests the discomfort that he had been experiencing due to the religions conflicts. It was, in fact, a great tragedy that he became a victim of religious hatred, for which he fought and suffered throughout his life.

Twenty years before assassination, Mahatma Gandhi said- he preferred 'Truth is God' to the phrase 'God is Truth' because although many people had been killed in the name of God, nobody had been killed in the name of truth.

Gandhi was the target of religious extremists, once on 20 January 1948 when an unsuccessful attempt was made on his life by a Hindu who took exception to his friendly overtures to Muslims. Yet, after this violent incident Gandhi said: 'You should not have any kind of hate against the person who was responsible for this. He took it for granted that I was an enemy of Hinduism.'

He successfully contested the advocates of hate and violence (whether against the British or between Hindus and Muslims) and sidelined them for over 60 years. Yet he was assassinated by one of those very extremists whom he had been trying to win over to the paths of peace and understanding.

Mahatama Gandhi's View on Religion

All Are God Given and True

I believe in the fundamental Truth of all great religions of the world. And I believe that if only we could, all of us, read the scriptures of the different Faiths from the standpoint of the followers of those faiths, we should find that they were at the bottom, all one and were all helpful to one another.

Belief in one God is the cornerstone of all religions. But I do not foresee a time when there would be only one religion on earth in practice. In theory, since there is one God, there can be only one religion.

The one religion is beyond all speech. Imperfect men put it into such language as they can command, and their words are interpreted by other men equally imperfect. Hence the necessity for tolerance, which does not mean indifference towards one's own Faith, but a more intelligent and pure love for it.

What Is Hinduism?

If were asked to define the Hindu creed, I should simply say: Search after Truth through non-violent means. A man may not believe even in God and still call himself a Hindu. Hinduism is a relentless pursuit after Truth and if today it has become moribund, inactive, irresponsive to growth, it is because we are fatigued and as soon as the fatigue is over Hinduism will burst forth upon the world with brilliance perhaps unknown before. Hinduism is the most tolerant of all religions. Its creed is all embracing.

Hinduism tells everyone to worship God according to his own Faith or Dharma and so it lives at peace with all the religions.

The Buddha's Contribution to Humanity

God's Laws are eternal and unalterable and not separable from God Himself. The Buddha disbelieved in God and simply believed in Moral Law. Great as Buddha's contribution to humanity was, in restoring God to His Eternal place, in my humble opinion, greater still was his contribution to humanity in his exacting regard of all life, be it ever so low.

The Message of Jesus

What does Jesus mean to me ? To me, He was one of the greatest teachers, humanity has ever had. To his believers, he was God's only begotten Son.

There is one thing which came to me in my early studies of the Bible. It seized me immediately. I read the passage: 'Make this world the Kingdom of God and His Righteousness and everything will be added unto you'.

I tell you that if you will understand, appreciate and act up to the spirit of this passage, you would not even need to know what place Jesus or any other teacher occupies in your heart. If you will.., clean and purify your hearts and get them ready, you will find that all these mighty Teachers will take their places without invitation from us. That, to my mind, is the basis of all sound education. Culture of mind must be subservient to the culture of the heart. May God help you to become pure?

The Distinctive Contribution of Islam

Islam's distinctive contribution to India's National Culture is its unadulterated belief in the Oneness of God and a practical application of the truth of the Brotherhood of Man for those who are nominally within its fold.

Real Religion Transcends All These Religions

Religion should pervade every one of our actions. Here religion does not mean sectarianism. It means a belief in ordered moral government of the universe. It is not less real because it is unseen. This religion transcends Hinduism, Islam, Christianity, etc. It does not supersede them. It harmonises them and gives them reality.

Religion Should Be Based On Humanity

Religion is to morality what water is to the seed that is sown in the soil. Just as the seed is choked under the earth when it is not duly watered, so too the morality which is devoid of the fertilising influence of religion gets thin and dry and is ultimately destroyed. In other words, morality divorced from religion would be an empty thing.

There is no religion higher than Truth and Righteousness. If we commit sins with the name of God on our lips, can we hope to win the grace of God? Suppose one man admits the existence of God, but lives a life of falsehood and immorality, while another knows not the name of God but lives a life of truth and virtue, can there be any doubt as to which should be regarded truly religious as well as moral?

Chapter-6

Gandhi's views on Islam and its practices

The word Islam means peace. And Peace is one of the names of 'Allah' (Quran 59:23). Islam is the religion which teaches 'Non-violence'. Quran says 'Allah' does not approve violence (Fasad). Fasad (Violence) is that action which result in destruction of social system causing loses in term of lives & property.s

Gandhi claimed that he had read the Quran more than once and also many other books on Quran and the Prophet Mohammad. (Gandhi, 1949: 235) He claimed he had read *Life of the Prophet* and also *Usva-e-Sahaba* and insisted that Islam never sanctioned destroying places of worship of other religions. (Gandhi, 1949: 139) He also claimed that the Prophet often fasted and prayed and that the Prophet had revelations not in moments of ease and luxurious living. Gandhi claimed that he had cultivated respect for Islam. (Gandhi, 1949:94) Gandhi ji clearly saw the difference between teaching and practices of Islam in Muslim community. He regarded Islam as a religion of peace. He claimed that there is nothing in the Quran to warrant the use of force for conversion. He also claimed that the holy book says in the clearest language possible that there is no compulsion in religion. He argued that Islam would cease to be a world religion if it were to rely upon force for its propagation (Gandhi, 1949:19). He had the view that Islam in the days of Harun-al- Rashid and Mamun was the most tolerant amongst the world's religions but there was a reaction against the liberalism of the teachers of their times. The reactionaries had many learned, able and influential men amongst them and they nearly overwhelmed the liberal and tolerant teachers and philosophers of Islam. He believed that Muslims are still suffering from the effect of that reaction, but he believed that Islam has sufficient in it to become purged of liberalism and intolerance (Gandhi, 1949:99).

Muslims argued with Gandhi claiming that he is wrong in saying that Islam enjoins non-violence upon its followers and that the Prophet himself met force with force at Badr. Muslims even argued that use of force is allowed on the particular occasions specified by Islam and especially against the non Muslim Government Islam prescribes only sword, protracted battle and the cutting of throat. (Gandhi, 1949: 261) Gandhi accepted that being a non Muslim he can always be challenged and hence is at a disadvantage while interpreting the Quran. However he argued that he was aware of the battle of ***Badr*** and similar incidents in the Prophet's life and also of the verses in the Quran that contradicted his claim of Islam being a peaceful religion. He asserted that it was possible that the teaching of a book or a man's life may be different from isolated texts in a book or incidents in a life. (Gandhi, 1949: 262) Same goes for the Quran and the Prophet and to Gandhi the central teaching of the Quran remained that of peace (Gandhi, 1949: 263). Gandhi acknowledged that some passages can be quoted from Quran which are contrary to peace. But he argued that same can be found in Christianity and Hinduism as well. He reasoned that we are all growing along with various religions. He acknowledged that the followers of Islam are too free with the sword, but in his opinion that was not because of teaching of Islam but due to the environment in which Islam was born. He argued that Islam is a comparatively new religion and is yet in the course of being interpreted. He rejected the claim of Maulvis to give a final interpretation to the message of the Mohamed (Gandhi, 1949:134).

He found Muslims to be brave, generous and trusting if their suspicions were disarmed (Gandhi, 1949: 62). He however acknowledged that in his experience he has found that Muslims are as a rule bully (Gandhi, 1949: 48). However he tried to explain this behaviour by stating that although non-violence has a predominant place in Quran, the 1300 years of imperialistic expansion has made the Muslims fighter as a body. They are therefore aggressive. Bullying is the natural excrescence of an aggressive spirit. Hence they have become bullies (Gandhi, 1949: 66). He claimed to have read Quran and to him it did not sanction or enjoin murder (Gandhi, 1949:125). He believed that Muslims have an ordeal to pass through. He cautioned that the sword is not an emblem of Islam, but clarified that Islam was born in an environment where the sword was and remains the supreme law. He lamented that the sword is too much in evidence among the Muslims despite the message of the Prophet. He advised that it must be sheathed if Islam is to be what it means - peace (Gandhi, 1949:131). He clarified that however good Islam may be in abstract the only way it can be judged is by the effect produced by each of its votaries considered as a whole (Gandhi, 1949: 63). He told the Muslims that they cannot protect Islam with the Lathi (stick) or sword. The age of Lathi (stick) is gone. A religion will be tested by the purity of its adherents. He argued that if a religion is left to the *Goondas* (criminals) to defend it, it will do serious harm to that religion including Islam. Islam will in that case no longer remain the faith of *fakirs* (mendicant monks) and worshippers of Allah (Gandhi, 1949:78). He objected to destruction of Hindu temples by Muslims (Gandhi, 1949:71). He acknowledged that he had found difficulty in the Muslim circles about invoking reverence for Hindu Vedas and incarnation (Gandhi, 1949:98). He expected Muslims to tolerate other religions. He reminded Muslims that Islam is judged by their conduct (Gandhi, 1949:72). However, he also argued that when a person of any religion does evil, it is an evil done by one person against another and each one should personally try to remove the evil because we are persons first and our religious identity is secondary. One should not blame the Muslims as a whole for some evil committed by a person or a group of persons. (Gandhi, 1949: 22). He explained that when blood boils, prejudice reigns supreme; man whether he labels himself a Hindu, Muslim, Christian or what not becomes a beast. (Gandhi, 1949:44) He advised that it is no use becoming angry with all Muslims in general. (Gandhi, 1949:24) He sought to gain Muslim friendship by right of love. (Gandhi, 1949: 26) In his characteristic non-violent arguments, he argued that if only one party were to continue its guilt and the other consistently remained patient and suffering the guilty party would be exhausted in the effort. If there is no reaction following the action the world would attain salvation (Gandhi, 1949:37). But if we answer an abuse with a slap a slap is returned with a kick, the kick than is returned by a bullet and so the circle of sin widens. But generally those who believe in taking a tooth for a tooth after a time forgive one another and become friends. So let us recognize this rule of mutual forgiveness and forget one another's wrongs. The easiest method of achieving peace is to give up the idea of complaining against one another and to concentrate our attention upon taking preventive measures so that there is no recurrence of madness (Gandhi, 1949: 38). He argued that religion is being interpreted in the lives of those who are living these messages in silence and in perfect self dedication. The seat of religion is in the heart. We have to write the interpretation of our respective faiths with our blood (Gandhi, 1949:135). He advised everyone to not force their views on one another. He argued that those who force others to respect their religious wishes are irreligious savages (Gandhi, 1949: 46). He argued that an attitude of non violence in mutual relations is an indispensable condition. People must not break each other's head in respect of religious matters (Gandhi, 1949: 47). He believed that Muslims alone are not to be blamed for everything in every place (Gandhi, 1949: 84) When he received reports of acts of violence by Muslims he investigated the facts before passing judgments (Gandhi, 1949: 55). He had to deal with cases in pre-independent India where Muslims had abducted Hindu boys and girls who were forced to embrace Islam. The remedy he suggested was non-violent resistance and if that is not possible than through most violent self-defence (Gandhi, 1949: 119). Ganidhi's ultimate remedy was to deal with the wrong but not to hurt the wrong doer.

(Gandhi, 1949:163). Thus to him the ultimate answer lay in the concept of 'Live and Let Live' or mutual forbearance and toleration in life. He claimed that this is the lesson he had learnt from the Quran. (Gandhi, 1949: 236). In his opinion, religion binds man to God and man to man and hence Islam binds not only Muslim to Muslim; but also Muslim to non-Muslims. The message of the Prophet was not just for Muslims and if anyone claims to the contrary he does greatest disservice to Islam and is poisoning the minds of Muslims (Gandhi, 1949: 310). In fact, when he was travelling to quell Hindu-Muslim riots in Bengal, he always carried the Gita, the *Quran* and the *Bible with him* (Gandhi, 1949:500.) He appealed to Muslims to do away with ' *Purdah* system' (Gandhi, 1949:502) .When some Muslims objected to this and said that Gandhi had no right to speak on Islamic Law, Gandhi countered by saying that this is a narrow view of religion. He hoped that this narrow view was not shared by other Muslims. He claimed the right to study and interpret the message of Islam. He said that Islam was not a creed to be preserved in a box. It was open to mankind to examine it and accept or reject its tenets. (Gandhi, 1949: 523) He also appealed that women folk should be rescued from the thraldom of ignorance and superstition (Gandhi, 1949: 506). He considered himself to be as good a Muslim as he was a Hindu and an equally good Christian and Parsi (Gandhi, 1949:538). During his prayer meetings, he always included verses from the *Quran Sharif.* He reminded people of folly of looking upon one religion as better than another (Gandhi, 1949: 585). Some people at times objected to recitation from the *Quran* when prayer meeting was being held in the Valmiki Temple.

He preferred not to hold the prayer meeting without the recitations from the *Quran* (Gandhi, 1949: 584). When some Muslims objected to his reading of Arabic verses from the ***Quran***, he refused to accept the objection. He asked why he cannot acclaim Mohammed as his Prophet (Gandhi, 1949:589). He advised both Hindus and Muslims to not look towards leaders for solutions but to look towards themselves and if they did than their desire for peace would be reflected by the leaders (Gandhi, 1949: 505). He quoted from the Prophet Mohammad that, "A perfect Muslim is he from whose tongue and hands mankind is safe. No man is true believer unless he desired for his brother that which he desired for himself. The most excellent ***Jehad*** is that for the conquest of self. Assist any person oppressed, whether Muslim or non-Muslim" (Gandhi, 1949:509). He welcomed inter-religious marriages with mutual friendship and respect for religion of each other (Gandhi, 1949: 542). He did not believe in state religion and opposed state aid to religious bodies. He only wanted schools to give ethical teachings as fundamental ethics were common to all religions (Gandhi, 1949: 543).

Chapter-7

Sufism and Gandhi

Sufism, known as 'Tasawwuf' in the Arabic-speaking world, is a form of Islamic mysticism that emphasizes introspection and spiritual closeness with God. ... **Sufi** practice focuses on the renunciation of worldly things, purification of the soul and the mystical contemplation of God's nature.

Sufism, mystical Islamic belief and practice in which Muslims seek to find the truth of divine love and knowledge through direct personal experience of God. ... Islamic mysticism is called 'Tasawwuf' (literally, "to dress in wool") in Arabic, but it has been called Sufism in Western languages since the early 19th century.

Non-Muslims often mistake Sufism as a sect of Islam. Sufism is more accurately described as an aspect or dimension of **Islam. Sufi** orders (Tariqas) can be found in Sunni, Shia and other Islamic groups.

Sufism is liberal Islam, with a colouring of Vedanta. Sufism is Islamic in origin. Sufism is the religion of love with Madhurya Bhava, with the concepts of the lover and the Beloved.

Sufism is not considered as an integral part of orthodox Islam. Other scholars have traced an Indian origin of the movement. Indian mysticism and Christian mysticism have affected the later developments of Sufism. Indian Sufism is a blend of Persian Sufism and Hindu mysticism.

Sufistic Saints

Lal Shahbaz, Mansoor, Shams Tabriez, Sachal, Rohal, Dalpat, Shah Inayet, Shah Latif, Bulleh Shah, Hafiz, Rumi and Jami were all Sufistic mystics.

The Sufistic saints are as liberal and catholic as the 'Vedantic Sannyasins'. They are mystic saints. They are devotional. Their utterances or sayings have a wonderful directness, freshness, spontaneous loveliness and charm.

The Sufi mystic sees the Lord in all. He experiences cosmic vision. He beholds his Beloved everywhere and in all objects. He has no sense of possession. He is free from egoism, lust, greed, anger and pride. He is perfectly passionless and enjoys perfect peace and poise. His state is beyond description. He is like the Jivanmukta, or liberated sage. He calls the heart as the palace of the Beloved. He does not care for dogmas or doctrines, creeds or sects. He has attained Para Bhakti or supreme devotion.

Doctrines

Asceticism is an essential feature of Sufism. The Sufi consecrates all his acts,-physical, mental and spiritual,-to the will of God. Unity of God, brotherhood of man and self-surrender to the Lord are the most vital doctrines of Sufism.

In Sufism God has form. The Sufis recognise His formless aspect too.

Tasawwuf (Sufism) combines ecstasy and service of man. A Sufi wants to remain in the world and serve humanity, but to be above worldliness.

The Sufi language of ecstasy describes the divine experience in a variety of ways such as sweetness, intoxication, perfume, sleep and death. Wine is a symbol of divine intoxication.

Absolute Bliss.

For a Sufi, music is a means to ecstasy. Music plays a very important part in Sufi religious exercise. Sufis worship beauty.

'Nasut' means the finite human qualities. 'Lahut' means the infinite qualities of God. Survival of individuality is 'Baqa.' 'Fana' means complete annihilation of the lower self or the mystical realisation of union with God. It means dying alive or the sublimation of the ego by annihilating it.

Sadhana

Concentration, meditation, obedience to a Guru (Pir), poverty, discipline, fasts, penances, Japa or recitation of the sacred word (Zikr), the use of rosary, rhythmic and controlled breathing, prayer, universal love, non-injury, detachment, introspection, dispassion, purity of heart and self-control are the means to attain God or the Beloved through divine grace.

The Sufi aspirant looks in a mirror and concentrates on the Trikute or the space between the two eye-brows in his own reflection in the mirror.

It is very difficult to practise the Bhava of the lover and the Beloved. This sort of Sufistic Sadhana proves dangerous in the case of unregenerate, passionate practitioners and leads to corruption. They mistake the intoxication caused by the drink of wine for Divine Intoxication and indulge themselves in drinking and sensuality. The aspirant should remain under the strict guidance of a Guru during his Sadhana period.

Words of Wisdom

Prayer carries us half-way to Allah; fasting, takes us to the door of His palace; charity gains us admission.

He needs no other rosary whose thread of life is strung with beads of love, service, charity and renunciation.

Righteousness is not that you turn your faces towards the east or the west, but a righteous man is one who believes in God, the last day, the angels, the Book and the prophets, who does charity to the poor, who is steadfast in prayer.

Happy are the believers, who humble themselves in prayer and who keep aloof from vain words, who do charitable acts, and who restrain their appetites. Your God is one God, there is no God but He, the Merciful, the Compassionate. Do good, because God loves those who do good.

Gandhi as Hindu Sufi sant:

Before assassination, Gandhi ji met son of Maulana Abul Bari Firangi Mahali at the shrine of the Sufi sant Qutbuddin Baktiyar Kaki. It had been the month of partition and the entire country was caught in communal riots when Mahatma Gandhi went on his fast unto death asking the riots to end. With the pressure of all sides to end the fast, he laid down conditions, of which the return to Kaki's shrine to Muslims and it be repaid by Hindu & Sikh together one.

Mahatama Gandhi's life was based on Truth, righteousness and non violence. He was believer of 'Sarvadharm Sambhav', which is similar to the essence of Sufism. Gandhi ji was Hindu but he was also firmly believer and practitioner of the equal respect to all religions, non-violence for peace and love to all, which fallows the doctrine of Sufism. Analysing the thoughts, life style and the conducts, I have no hesitation to say that Gandhi ji was Hindu Sufi sant.

Chapter-8

Secularism & Gandhi

What is Secularism?

Secularism, also called Secularity, is the idea of something being not religious or not connected to a worship or worship place like Church, Mosque, Mandir, Gurdwara etc. An example of this is the government, which is independent of any religion in many states.

Secularism is a principal that involve two basic proportions-

- Strict separation of the state from religious institutions.
- People of different religions and belief are equal before Law.

Secularism is the principal of the separation of government institutions and religious dignitaries. One manifestation of secularism is asserting the rights to be free from religious rule and teachings, or, in a state declared to be neutral on matter of belief, from imposition by government of religion or religious practices upon its people.

Another manifestation is the view that public activities and decisions, especially one, should be uninfluenced by religious belief and/ or practice

In the West, the word **secular** implies three things: freedom of religion, equal citizenship to each citizen regardless of his or her religion, and the separation of religion and state. ... It means equal treatment of all religions. Religion in **India** continues to assert its political authority in matters of personal law.

Definitions:

- Indifference to, or rejection or exclusion of, religion and religious considerations (Merriam-Webster)
- The belief that religion should not be involved with the ordinary social and political activities of a country (Cambridge Dictionary)
- The principle of separation of the state from religious institutions (Oxford Dictionaries)
- A system of social organization and education where religion is not allowed to play a part in civil affairs (Collins)
- A theory, belief, ideology, or political modality that demarcates the secular from other phenomena (usually religious) and prioritizes the secular over the non-secular in some regard.

In political terms, secularism is a movement towards the separation of religion and government (often termed the separation of church and state). This can refer to reducing ties between a government and a state religion, replacing laws based on scripture (such as Halakha, Dominionism, and Sharia law) with civil laws, and eliminating discrimination on the basis of religion. This is said to add to democracy by protecting the rights of religious minorities.

Some scholars have argued that the separation of worship places (church etc.) and state is but one possible strategy to be deployed by secular governments. What all secular governments, from the democratic to the authoritarian, share is a concern about the relationship between the church and the state. Each secular government may find its own unique policy prescriptions for dealing with that concern (separation being one of those possible policies; French models, in which the state carefully monitors and regulates the church, being another).

Secular Society

In studies of religion, modern democracies are generally recognized as secular. This is due to the near-complete freedom of religion and the lack of authority of religious leaders over political decisions.

Modern sociology has, since Max Weber, often been preoccupied with the problem of authority in secularized societies and with secularization as a sociological or historical process.

Some societies become increasingly secular as the result of social processes, rather than through the actions of a dedicated secular movement; this process is known as secularization.

Sociologist Peter L. Berger maintained that the modern world can no longer be described as being secular or becoming increasingly secular; instead it can best be described as being pluralistic.

Secular Ethics

Secularism is a code of duty pertaining to this life, founded on considerations purely human, and intended mainly for those who find theology indefinite or inadequate, unreliable or unbelievable. Its essential principles are three: (1) The improvement of this life by material means. (2) That science is the available Providence of man. (3) That it is good to do good. Whether there be other good or not, the good of the present life is good, and it is good to seek that good.

Contemporary ethical debate in the West is often described as "secular." The work of well known moral philosophers such as Derek Parfit and Peter Singer and even the whole field of contemporary bioethics have been described as explicitly secular or non-religious.

The principles of secularism which protect and underpin many of the freedoms we enjoy are:

1. Separation of religious institutions from state institutions and a public sphere where religion may participate, but not dominate.
2. Freedom to practice one's faith or belief without harming others, or to change it or not have one, according to one's own conscience.
3. Equality so that our religious beliefs or lack of them doesn't put any of us at an advantage or a disadvantage.

Separation of religion from state

The separation of religion and state is the foundation of secularism. It ensures religious groups don't interfere in affairs of state, and the state doesn't interfere in religious affairs.

Christianity is one major influence among many that shape our current ways of life. We are a nation of many denominations and religions. Large sectors of the population do not hold or practice, religious beliefs.

If Britain were truly a secular democracy, political structures would reflect the reality of changing times by separating religion from the state.

Secularism protects both believers and non-believers

Secularism seeks to ensure and protect freedom of religious belief and practice for all citizens. Secularists want freedoms of thought and conscience to apply equally to all – believers and non-believers alike. They do not wish to curtail religious freedoms.

Religious Freedom

Secularism seeks to defend the absolute freedom of religious and other belief, and protect the right to manifest religious belief insofar as it does not impinge on the rights and freedoms of others. Secularism ensures that the right of individuals to freedom of religion is always balanced by the right to be free from religion.

Secularism is about democracy and fairness

In a secular democracy all citizens are equal before the law and parliament. No religious or political affiliation gives advantages or disadvantages and religious believers are citizens with the same rights and obligations as anyone else.

Secularism champions universal human rights above religious demands. It upholds equality laws that protect women, LGBT people and minorities from religious discrimination. These equality laws ensure that non-believers have the same rights as those who identify with a religious or philosophical belief.

Equal access to public services

We all, share hospitals, schools, the police and the services of local authorities. It is essential that these public services are secular at the point of use, so no-one is disadvantaged or denied access on grounds of religious belief (or non-belief). All state-funded schools should be non-religious in character, with children being educated together regardless of their parents' religion. When a public body grants a contract for the provision of services to an organization affiliated to a particular religion or belief, such services must be delivered neutrally, with no attempt to promote the ideas of that faith group.

Secularism is not atheism

Atheism is a lack of belief in gods. Secularism simply provides a framework for a democratic society. Atheists have an obvious interest in supporting secularism, but secularism itself does not seek to challenge the tenets of any particular religion or belief, neither does it seek to impose atheism on anyone.

Secularism is simply a framework for ensuring equality throughout society – in politics, education, the law and elsewhere – for believers and non-believers alike.

Secularism protects free speech and expression

Religious people have the right to express their beliefs publicly but so do those who oppose or question those beliefs. Religious beliefs, ideas and organizations must not enjoy privileged protection from the right to freedom of expression. In a democracy, all ideas and beliefs must be open to discussion. Individuals have rights; ideas do not.

Secularism is the best chance we have to create a society in which people of all religions or none can live together fairly and peacefully.

Gandhi's Secularism and India

Gandhi's secular theories took on a special significance in the particular context of the Indian national movement. Indian society has been traditionally plagued by the evils of caste and creed based discrimination. The caste oriented stratification of the Indian society has hindered all chances of national unification from the early days of Indian society. The situation was complicated by the presence of various religious groups within the country, who were not ready to compromise any ground to reach a platform of commonality. The traditional rhetoric of the religious and the self-styled spiritual preachers fuelled these divisions more often than not. It was a great pain for Gandhi that India's age old tradition of religious tolerance was not being maintained when it was more needed. What particularly disturbed him was the realization that it would be impossible to organize any nationwide movement against the common opposition of the British oppressors, if society continues to remain divided on religious grounds. Secularism for Gandhi was an absolute necessity to bring about any form of constructive and all-encompassing political movement.

Gandhi preached his ideals of secularism and religious tolerance across the length and breadth of the country. He showed his consolidation to the Muslim leaders through the support that Congress extended to the ***Khilafat*** movement. Gandhi wrote extensively on the need of secularism in India, and made speeches to the same effect all over the country.

It was not the easiest of tasks for Gandhi. The British were bent upon implementing the policy of divide and rule, and it took its worst form after the declaration of separate elections for the different communities in the declaration of the Government of India Act in 1935. Indian National movement has always been plagued by communal tensions, and haunted it till the very end. Gandhi's monumental efforts at bringing together the various communities in India were not fully realized. The British policy of 'divide and rule' had its effects, and the demand for a separate Muslim nation was fast gaining currency. Gandhi was hurt, but he realized his helplessness. Even at the intense riots on the eve of Indian independence, Gandhi was on the roads trying to unite the warring communal factions. Even his death can in many ways be related to his life-long commitment to secular principles.

Maharaja Ranjeet Singh of the Sikh empire of the first half of the 19th century successfully established a secular rule in the Punjab. This secular rule respected members of all races and religions and it allowed them to participate without discrimination in his Darbar. He had Sikh, Muslim and Hindu representatives heading the Darbar. Ranjit Singh also extensively funded education, religion, and arts of various different religions and languages.

In accord with the belief in the separation of church and state, secularists tend to prefer that politicians make decisions for secular rather than religious reasons.

❍❍❍

Chapter-9

Hindu Muslim Unity

Mahatma Gandhi Views on Cordial Hindu-Muslim Relations!

Going through Mahatma Gandhi's autobiography, time to time guidance given to his followers and speeches delivered in public meetings he always emphasised on Hindu Muslim unity to achieve Independence of India from British rule. He was very clear that unity of all the religion can only make the India as a Nation. Analysing the letters written by Mahatma Gandhi to different personalities and in response to people's queries he always shows his deep concern on Hindu Muslim Unity to make the movement of Independence strong. He always tried to resolve the problems of Muslim community and encouraged them to come forward.

In Gandhi's view, in addition to swadeshi and the removal of untouchability, the necessity of cordial relations between Hindus and Muslims was a leading factor in the social progress of the country. He made this issue, too, an essential component of the constructive programme launched in 1920. Though he did not sponsor a specific movement for the purpose, he repeatedly suggested, in word and action, ways and means of promoting communal harmony. On several occasions, Gandhi was able, through individual action and sheer force of personality, to bring communal riots to an immediate halt. Social and political change could not be planned without taking this factor into consideration, according to him.

Gandhi's long and lively association with both Muslims and Hindus in South Africa had made him conscious of the fact that both had much in common and their traditional harmony, which had been somewhat fractured in the preceding decades, could be re-established in India. He perceived the Khilafat demand as presenting an excellent opportunity for bringing the Muslim masses into the national struggle for freedom and for restoring amicable relations between Hindus and Muslims.

Gandhi asked the leaders to submit a calm, dispassionate and reasoned statement of the Mahommedan claim to the British authorities. Till then, though pro-Khilafat sentiments had been running high among the Muslims, there had been no organized plan of action on the issue. Through discussions, Gandhi persuaded the Khilafat leaders to chalk out a national programme of non-violent action.

He obviously estimated that if non-Muslims joined the Muslims on the Khilafat issue, it would be a big step towards the emotional integration of the country.

Gandhi was aware of Muslim reservations about the issue of non-violence as a technique of agitation, but after several consultations with Maulana Abdul Bari, who commanded wide influence, he managed to persuade him and others of its necessity. He published letters in leading newspapers and his own journals on the justice of the Khilafat issue. Important leaders such as Moti Lal

Nehru, C.R. Das, Swami Shraddhanand and Bamanji of Saharanpur gave him full support.

In November 1919, the Khilafat demand was made an issue of the all India satyagraha campaign that had been launched that April. This was the first major step taken by Gandhi to bring about Hindu-Muslim harmony and identify common issues between the two communities. Gandhi's impact on the Muslims can be judged from the conduct of Maulana Abdul Bari, who began preaching about the need to stop cow slaughter out of regard for Hindu sensibilities. On 6 September 1919, when Bakri Eid was being celebrated, he wired Gandhi: "In celebration of Hindu-Muslim unity, no cow sacrifices in Firangi Mahal this Bakrid – Abdul Bari."

Unfortunately, the phase of communal harmony that began in 1919 proved to be short-lived. Turkey itself made the Khilafat question redundant by abolishing the sultanate in 1924. Thus, the focal point of Hindu-Muslim political cooperation disintegrated. Communal riots broke out soon after the withdrawal of the non-cooperation movement in February 1922 and continued sporadically till 1924, when Gandhi morally compelled the communities to sign a truce in his own unique way – through a fast.

Gandhi felt himself responsible for the unprecedented scale of communal violence because it followed a period of communal cooperation initiated by him. He began his 21 day penitential fast on 17 September 1924 in the house of his close friend, Mohammad Ali, as a visible demonstration of his love for the Muslims. Gandhi perceived his own role in the following manner: "I am striving to become the best cement between the two communities. My longing is to be able to cement the two with my blood, if necessary."

The upshot of his fast was that Hindus and Muslims got together and held a unity conference in Delhi on 26 and 27 September 1924 and passed a resolution drafted by Gandhi. This resolution was remarkable for its contents because it showed a genuine effort by both parties to re-establish a friendly atmosphere. It deplored the cruelties perpetrated during the riots and stated that it was "unlawful and irreligious for any person to take the law into his own hands".

The conference was of the opinion that all differences should be referred to arbitration or a court of law. A board of arbitrators was appointed. On the controversial issues of cow slaughter and the playing of music before mosques, it was agreed that neither Hindus nor Muslims should use force, but rely on each other's good sense and the growth of better relations between them. Newspapers and pamphlets that inflamed communal passions came in for sharp criticism and the board of arbitrators was asked to scrutinize such writings from time to time and publish correct versions.

Another important achievement of this conference was that it authorized the board of arbitrators to frame a scheme for the protection of the rights of minorities and, for this purpose, invited representatives from all parties and all sections of society. The scheme, it was proposed, would be published and be binding on all parties for a period of five years ending in 1929, when it would be revised by a joint conference representing all interests.

On the subject of religious conversions, the resolution stated that tabligh or shuddhi of minors or adults without education and clear understanding was contrary to moral sense and should be abandoned. Every conversion must be done openly and after notice to the relatives of the people concerned."

As in other spheres, Gandhi had great expectations of women being able to play a positive role in the betterment of inter-communal relations. He had been deeply impressed by their powers of suffering and sacrifice during the civil disobedience movement. He asked them to use the weapon of 'satyagraha' now to secure Hindu-Muslim unity.

They should, he advised, not cooperate with the men at home and starve themselves and their men till they gave up communal squabbles. "Assure me of your cooperation," he said, "and you will add tremendously to my strength and to my power of pleading."

Another approach Gandhi tried was to draw the influential classes among the Muslims into the sphere of national and social development. In a speech at the Jamiat-ul-Ulema Conference in Karachi on 1 April 1931, he asked the delegate ulema to use their influence with the masses to propagate non-violent methods in resolving disputes, just as he was doing among the general public.

He also appealed to the ulema to set an example by adopting the nationwide programme of swadeshi and give up their love of imported cloth. Muslim zamindars could also do their bit, Gandhi believed, in improving relations with their Hindu neighbours. His message was especially for those in the province of Sindh, where they were feared and distrusted by the Hindus. A successful experiment in Sindh would be easily, emulated in the other provinces, he thought.

In searching for a more enduring solution to the problem of communal riots, Gandhi mooted the idea of forming Peace Brigades. But their members had to have certain qualifications, according to him. Among these were a living faith in non-violence and equal regard for all the principal religions of the world. They were required to be local men and women who would cultivate, through personal service, contacts with people in their locality so that they were trusted by them.

They would thus be in a position to anticipate trouble and deal with it accordingly. They would also need to be in such occupations as to leave them leisure for this sort of voluntary service. He suggested that they should wear a distinctive dress so that they would be easily recognized. It hardly needs to be said that such peace brigades could render valuable service in any part of the world.

Though Gandhi's efforts to establish Hindu-Muslim unity did not succeed in the long run due to many extraneous factors, it cannot be denied that his lack of bias, his zeal for establishing harmonious relations between different sections of India's population, and his personal integrity won him the love and trust of important segments of the Muslim community.

Chapter-10

Gandhi's approach to Communal harmony

Gandhi was undoubtedly a great person having very complex personality. He had to deal with a complex society of a diverse country, India, and had to deal with Britain. Gandhi was deeply religious yet so rational. It was difficult to lead Indian society without understanding its religious and cultural ethos. Gandhi did not ignore the religious sentiments of the people of India. Indian people were deeply influenced by religion, culture, customs and traditions. It was, therefore, necessary for an effective leader to emphasize the role of reason. Thus Gandhi combined religiosity with reason and talked of letting in fresh winds from the west by keeping mental, windows open. Thus to westernized people, he appeared to be too religious and too superstitiously religious to be rational.

And it was due to such a complex character that Gandhi became a great leader. He responded to all developing situations very carefully and intelligently. In view of certain calamitous situations he would become enigmatically silent and would speak only after a number of days spending periods of silence for deep reflection. He never acted instinctively. Many of his actions appeared to be quite enigmatic, even to his close followers like Nehru and others. Nehru was baffled when the Mahatma withdrew the civil disobedience movement when it was at its height afterthe Chauri Chaura incident. But Gandhi withdrew the movement as it was becoming violent and he knew once violence starts it will go totally out of control and the British rulers will suppress it ruthlessly.

He took up the Khilafat movement in 1919, which appeared even to Jinnah as pandering to sectarian mullahs and he differed from Gandhi on this question. But Gandhi knew the deeper urges of the Muslims of India and by supporting the Khilafat movement he successfully drew Muslim masses into the freedom movement and the Jami's-at-ul-Ulama-I-Hind (an organization of Muslim theologians of India), became a permanently of Indian National Congress.

Gandhi was a man of the masses, Gandhi drew masses into the freedom supporting the Khilafat movement he successfully drew Muslim masses into the freedom movement and the Jami's-at-ul-Ulama-I-Hind (an organization of Muslim theologians of India), became a permanently of Indian National Congress.

Gandhi was a man of the masses; Gandhi drew masses into the freedom movement. Gandhi was a fighter for the cause.

Gandhi developed the doctrine of Satyagraha and nonviolence which was unique in the modern political movements. He elevated it to the status of a political doctrine.

The twentieth and twenty first centuries so far have been the most violent and the world needs the doctrine of nonviolence as never before. In this respect Gandhi remains most relevant. He proved the efficacy of nonviolent political struggle and while all other colonial countries were waging armed struggles for freedom, India was the only country fighting for its liberation through nonviolent means. Gandhi, though himself, a Hindu, was not an exclusivist. He was not only inclusivist but also the upholder of the doctrine of pluralism. He firmly believed in the principle of equal respect for all religions of the world. For Sufis the basic doctrines are sulh-I-kul (total peace or peace with all) and love (Muhabhat). Also, like the Sufis, he believed in living a simple life, a life based on needs, not on greed. He often pointed out there is enough on this earth for everyone's need and not enough even for one man's greed.

Gandhi ji were deeply committed to Indian Pluralism and human rights and individual dignity. He was aware and appreciative of the contribution to Indian culture by all communities, particularly of Muslims. Gandhi was indeed deeply aware of the Muslim question. He wanted to tackle it with a sense of justice and wisdom. He was exclusivist to the core. He knew the nation could not be built by excluding the Muslims at any level; it enormously complicated the communal problem. The Hindu communal forces too believed in Hindu Rashtra and considered Muslims as alien and at best secondary citizens. The RSS theorists had laid the foundation of separate nationhood much before Jinnah did. Lala Lajpat Rai, Bhai Parmanand, Veer Savarkar and Hedgevar, all believe Hindu.

Mahasabha leaders and RSS leaders hated Gandhi because of his emphasis on love and nonviolence and respect for other religions.

Gandhi firmly believed in secular nationalism and unity of the country.

The Hindu Rashtravadis, though they talked of Akhand Bharat and never tired of talking of patriotism, were, in fact, responsible for the vivisection of the country. They hated Muslims, the largest minority and considered them as aliens. They thought, highly superficially of course, that Muslims could never be true patriots (though they themselves were not). Thus through this approach they strengthened the hands of separatists among Muslims and made it obvious for these Muslim separatists that the two nation theory was justified and that Hindus and Muslims indeed cannot live together. This proved disastrous for the unity and integrity of our country.

Gandhi, on the other hand, believed in tolerance and acceptance of all religions within the Indian national framework. A modern nation state, he knew, could not be built on intolerance towards others and by excluding them. Nationhood cannot be based on religion. It will only lead to intolerance, hatred and violence. Religious nationalism can and does lead to fascistic tendencies. All communal forces whether of Muslim or the Hindu variety hated Gandhi precisely because tolerance, love and nonviolence which would totally negate religious nationalism and exclusivist approach. Religious nationalism can be sustained only on hatred and violence. Religious nationalists hate nonviolence and peace. They thrive on hatred and violence.

In fact religious nationalism is nothing but gross misuse of both, religion and nationalism. A true love of religion and a true patriot would never allow such misuse, either of religion or of the concept of a nation. A communalist, though he projects himself as a patriot, is not. Similarly he thinks he is the defender of his religion but it is not so. One who hates a section of people of his own country cannot be a patriot in any sense of the word and one who peddles hate in the name of religion cannot be truly religious. The communalists are hate mongers on one hand, and champions of their vested interests on the other. It is also important to note that communalists cannot be democrats either. They do not believe in democratic dissent. Anyone who disagrees is a traitor to the 'cause'. Gandhi, on the other hand, was deeply religious, truly patriotic and a great democrat. His politics was based on values like truth and nonviolence. A democracy, in order to be meaningful has to imbibe these values. For Gandhi, the cow was a holy animal as he was an orthodox Hindu. Yet nonviolence was more important to him than the cow. Thus he writes in Young India (May 7, 1919) "I believe myself to be an orthodox Hindu and it is my conviction that no one who scrupulously practices the Hindu religion may like a cow killer to protect the cow." And in Young - India (May 18, 1921) he wrote very insightfully, "To attempt cow protection by violence is to reduce Hinduism to Satanism and to prostitute to a base end the grand significance of cow protection." He further says in the same issue, "The Hindu must scrupulously refrain from using any violence against the Mussalman. Suffering and trust are attributes of soul force. I have heard that, at big fairs, if a Mussalman is found in possession of cows or even goats, he is at times forcibly dispossessed. Those claiming to be Hindus, thus resort to violence and are enemies of the cow and of Hinduism."

In our own times we witness that VHP and Bajarang Dal activists openly inciting violence against Muslims and Dalits. Several riots have taken place in India in the post independence period too, on this question. What happened in Jhajjar, Haryana a year ago is a hair raising event. Four dalits who were skinning dead cows were lynched. Thus, as pointed out above, communalists can never be truly religious. Gandhi boldly states that it is not Hinduism but 'Satanism'. It is a very harsh word but, for Gandhi, anyone using violence amounts to an act of Satan.

For Gandhi truth and non violence are the fundamentals for every religion and he calls them to be the master key with which the essence of every religion is to be unlocked. A communalist, however, never accepts truth and nonviolence. His creed is violence and falsehood. For him revenge is far more fundamental than forgiving. Gandhi was against retaliation as it involves violence. He stood for forgiveness rather than revenge. He wrote in Young India of August 18, 1924, "The law of retaliation has been tried since the day of Adam and we know from experience that it has hopelessly failed. We are groaning under its poisonous effect. Above all, the Hindus may not break mosques in retaliation against temples that are broken. That way lies slavery and worse. Even though a thousand temples may be reduced to bits, I would not touch a single mosque and expect thus to prove the superiority of my faith to the so called faith of fanatics."A communalist can never accept such superior morality. His actions are based on feelings of revenge.

Gandhi was greatly concerned with the weakest and poorest people and his real measure of progress was how much the weakest sections of society have gained from it. Nehru developed the concept of mixed economy to cater to the needs of the poorer sections of society.

❍ ❍ ❍

Chapter-11

Gandhi & Peace

Gandhi's Principal for Peace:

Mahatma Gandhi is the greatest apostle of peace, the world has seen after Buddha and Christ. His notion of peace is centered on nonviolence, individualism, soul force and forgiveness. At first glance, *global peace* initiatives might be perceived as far-flung methodologies that have wholly diverged from his ideologies.

The quintessential qualities of justice and peace that made *Mahatma Gandhi* the man who changed our world for the better with his ideals of faith, love and tolerance. *Mahatma Gandhi* taught us that we can bring harmony to our **world** by becoming champions of love and peace for all.

In Gandhi's theory of peace, human values take great prominence. Nonviolence (Ahimsa) is a way of life rather than a tactic, and, together with the search for truth (Satyagraha), makes the difference between passive submission to injustice, and an active struggle against it. This struggle excludes both physical violence and casting the opponent in the role of enemy, and hence presupposes compassion and self-criticism. The notion of welfare to all (Sarvodaya) also sees peace as incompatible with exploitation or inequality of wealth. Peace is not seen as an end state, but as a continuous revolutionary process, where ends cannot be separated from means.

Gandhi's vision on Peace:

Gandhi ji maintained that there cannot be true and lasting peace unless there is equal opportunity for all:

"You cannot have a good social system when you find yourself low in the scale of political rights, nor can you be fit to exercise political rights and privileges unless your social system is based on reason and justice. You cannot have a good economic system when your social arrangements are imperfect. If your religious ideas are low and groveling, you cannot succeed in ensuring equal status for women, and the access to opportunities for all is the ultimate that would bring independence to the people of India."

So when we talk of peace as Gandhiji saw it, we have to look for comprehensive solutions. I perceive the lessons from Gandhiji's life as being three-fold:

The goal of the struggle for peace and democracy is for the good of all; not just the good of the majority.

That one has to be prepared to make sacrifices to attain this. That political power in itself does not result in peace and democracy; we have to work and strive for peace and democracy. Locating these lessons within our situation today, it becomes clear that we have a long and steep road ahead.

Gandhiji's life has taught us one very clear lesson: it is easy to postulate principles, but very difficult to put them into practice. Believing in peace and a good life for all is very well but the final step is putting into practice what we have learnt or begun to believe in. This final step is what eventually determines the quality of our lives. There are many questions which have been brought before the

Goldstone Commission about the violence in our country. The questions of political violence, the question of police and army violence, the question of the "third force", the question of tribal or ethnic violence, and so on. Yet the structural violence caused by the non-provision of adequate water, sanitation, medical care, housing and social security — all of which lead to the deaths of thousands of our people weekly — has not been addressed.

When Gandhiji came to South Africa he saw that the people had acquiesced to the harsh treatment to which they were subjected. The indentured workers chose to run away from their contracts or to commit suicide as a result of the harsh treatment meted out to them by their employers. In India the poor farm workers suffered similar treatment and had also given in to these conditions. Gandhiji instilled in them dignity and a sense of direction. He raised their consciousness about their rights and aroused in them a will to resist the oppression they suffered.

The struggle for liberation in South Africa also drew the same response from the people as did the defiance campaigns of Gandhiji. Thousands of people took to the streets to draw attention to their plight. It is ironic that in South Africa such mass action is seen as violent while the brutality in the townships and the loss of thousands of lives have aroused little reaction from the authorities. We see frantic attempts to get parties to sign peace accords, yet many fundamental concerns of the people remain unaddressed. As we draw to the close of the 20th century — no matter how promising the negotiations may be — peace in South Africa and world peace are indeed pressing issues. So perhaps Gandhiji's life is more relevant and significant today than ever before.

Having political power is therefore just the first step towards peace. We all have to accept the responsibility to change things. We have a responsibility to cultivate some of the principles by which Gandhiji lived. We have to begin to look at sharing and ensuring that resources are distributed equitably. We must ensure that people can see and feel the change and be able to identify a niche for themselves in the world. In addition to political oppression, we have economic, intellectual, religious, environmental, and gender oppression in South Africa. When we talk about peace, we cannot view the indiscriminate killings and destruction of property in isolation from the poverty, illiteracy, religious intolerance, environmental threats and gender oppression faced by our people. But having identified problems, it is also necessary to look for solutions. It is clear that change of political power in itself will not be able to achieve peace. De Klerk certainly needs to rethink the whole notion of enforced peace. So what can we do to achieve peace in our country? How can we help to build a society where peace will be the central concern of all its people? I think that Gandhiji would consider the following as essential conditions for peace: That people in power, whether political, economic, religious, civic or administrative power, need to develop a holistic view of peace. If we want a better country for our grandchildren and great-grandchildren then we need to act and ensure that such a holistic view is adopted and that a comprehensive approach is used in addressing the issue of peace. We also have a responsibility to ensure that the community understands and approves of this approach. We must be willing to share expertise and funds, and at the same time develop the community's capacity to meet the challenges of the future.

We cannot expect a new government to change things on its own. We have to take responsibility for bringing about changes and in this we can seek the assistance of the state. We need to develop a climate of love, caring, sharing and communal consciousness as we begin the process of building an equitable society through community programmes. We certainly may be able to get more support for such projects from a new government. We need to build a culture of non-violence among our children and youth, through actively ensuring that we (and they) do not support war toys or violent games, media, books, stories, etc., but instead promote a culture of resistance to injustice.

We need to inculcate a communal responsibility among all our people. We need to create a culture of work, and recognise the dignity of work, so that we can learn not only to meet our own needs but also those of the whole community. We need to develop a South African identity, so that we can be rid of the racism and sexism embedded in us through life under apartheid and begin to love our people and our country. We should be vigilant to the needs of the community and begin to lay the foundation for a more equitable society where everyone may have access to opportunities. The present unemployment situation needs to be seriously challenged and work opportunities created for all people. These are the goals Gandhiji set for development work in India and I guess they apply to us today. Perhaps only when these goals have been achieved, will we be able to say to ourselves that we have achieved peace in our country, a peace for which Gandhiji lived, worked, and died.

Models of Structuring Peace and Gandhi in Modern Democratic System:

The concept of world peace has been fascinating indeed. Gandhi realised that if the embodied human spirit was to progress, muffled as it was by selfish desire, man must be free, full of dignity and earnest about his own advance. "There has been no greater advocate of one humanity, one world and no stronger opponent of violence and war than Gandhi, for, his faith in no-violence was absolute and he believed that peaceful means alone could lead to peaceful ends " 'While world peace is undoubtedly one of the most universal and significant of human ideals, Gandhi has described is as 'one of the few positive symbols having meaning for the whole of humanity' The present world is beset with problems like international terrorism, arms race, civil wars and ethnic and religious problems. Though cold war is over, there are smaller conflicts between and among nations. These regional conflicts have disturbed international peace, attempts for disarmaments, confidence building measure etc. The twentieth century was by far the bloodiest and most destructive century in the history of the human race. According to UN statistics, there were only twenty eight days in this entire century of genocide and destruction without a war of some kind, in some part of the globe.

Mahatma Gandhi has always spoken about structuring peace throughout his life. Gandhi showed the world not only the goal of peace but the supreme method of achieving world peace. George C Marshall writes, "In his devotion to structuring peace and tolerance of the brotherhood the Mahatma was one of those rare spokesman for the conscience of all mankind." Structuring peace and tolerance, for Gandhi, were the supreme means for the realisation of Truth and Love which were identical to the Ultimate End of man. Gandhi developed his world-view against the background of a world of violence. Paying tribute to Mahatma Gandhi on his 75th birthday, Albert Einstein wrote: "Generations to come, it may well be, will scarcely believe that such a one as this ever in flesh and blood walked upon this earth ". Gandhi today has become a universal symbol more than anything else of the supreme principles of truth, love, non-violence, justice and human brotherhood. It is precisely a desire to bridge this gap between the 'ideal' and the 'real' that attracts researchers to the peace programme.

Structuring Peace through Coercive Power:

The first peace paradigm, power politics or 'realpolitik', is the traditionally dominant framework in the field of international relations. This paradigm, grounded in classic works such as Thucydides' History of the Peloponnesian War as well as in a more recent body of political theory. There is a very popular saying that "Villains don't fall from the skies, neither do they pop out of the ground like evil spirits. They must be seen as symptoms of society and therefore every citizen is responsible for their existence [4]". Violence arises inevitably from human competitiveness and covetousness; peace is secured through the forceful imposition of order.

Structuring Peace through Mutual Understanding:

The second paradigm, conflict resolution, offers a highly pragmatic approach to peace through the development and refinement of skills for analyzing conflicts and responding to them with effective strategies of communication and negotiation. According to this paradigm, conflict is a natural at all levels of human interaction and organisation, from inter-personal to the inter-ethnic and international. To manage and resolve conflicts effectively, we must become aware of our attitudes towards conflict and our habitual conflict management style so as to attain greater freedom to define our responses in a proactive and coordinated way. Such awareness increases our chances of achieving "win-win" rather than "win-lose" or "lose-lose" solutions. We learn to understand and work with our own emotions, to generate openness to more authentic communication, and to control processes that might otherwise lead to escalation.

It would seem to be a reasonable assumption that Gandhi's well publicised examples of non-violence resistance and the voluminous writings on his technique at least set the tone for the later development and phenomenal growth of conflict resolution literature in the guise of modern problem-solving and win-win approaches leading to integrative conflict resolution.

Structuring International Peace through Power of Law:

The third approach to peace explored by the class is the world order paradigm. This paradigm, which views the 'order' created by practices of power politics as a form of disorder, proposes that sustained cooperation among states and other significant factors, such as nongovernmental organisations and inter-governmental organisations is both possible and necessary. Co-operation is possible because human nature contains the potential for both selfishness and altruism.

To affirm that principled co-operation is possible, the world order paradigm emphasizes human choice and intentionally while asserting that nation-states do not have a monopoly on power to shape global politics. The nation-state is not the only forum for political activity and accountability, and the national interest is not the exclusive criterion for desirable behaviour. In an age of globalisation, politics involves a complex interplay of global and national as well as local loyalties, values and interests. Modern communications and transportation technologies have empowered citizens to form transportation networks for advancing concerns linked to peace, human rights, ecology and development.

Structuring Peace through Mediation:

The final approach to peacemaking investigated in the peace paradigms course is the transformation paradigm, a paradigm that focuses on the centrality of education, cultural change and spirituality in all genuine attempts to make peace a reality in daily life. From the standpoint of the transformation paradigm, peacemaking is not only an effort to end war, remove structural violence, or establish the presence of external value conditions. It is also a profoundly internal process, in which the transformation is individual becomes a metaphor for an instrument of broader changes. Peaceful behaviour is a learned behaviour, and each individual is a potential and needed contributor to a culture of peace.

Mahatma Gandhi takes real democracy to be that admits governmental interference all the minimum, which has peace at the maximum and all progress on the basis of equality. It is possible only when non-violence is imparted the supreme status in practice as well as in principle and at social as well as individual plane. Only such a democracy can be successful in its real goal.

Gandhian Concept of Peace and Satyagraha:

Nonviolence (Ahimsa) is a way of life rather than a tactic, and, together with the search for truth (Satyagraha), makes the difference between passive submission to injustice, and an active struggle against it. This struggle excludes both physical violence and casting the opponent in the role of enemy, and hence presupposes compassion and self-criticism. The notion of welfare to all (sarvodaya) also sees peace as incompatible with exploitation or inequality of wealth. Peace is not seen as an end state, but as a continuous revolutionary process, where ends cannot be separated from means.

Satyagraha is Gandhi's technique of non-violent activism. The term has variously been translated as 'passive resistance', 'non-violent resistance', 'non-violent direct action' and even 'militant non-violence'. For Gandhi, it was not only a method of conducting conflict but it was also a way of life, living in truth. From the standpoint view of nonviolence activists, this assumption reflects the dominance of ability to hurt and therefore regard it as the exclusive possession of governments and armed militant groups.

In response, the non-violence paradigm proposes that the power of any government derives primarily from the consent of the people, and only secondarily from coercion. By consenting to any given state of affairs and operating within the framework of norms that it offers, human beings empower that order and, if its norms are dehumanising, disempowered and dehumanise themselves. In Gandhi's theory of peace, human values take great prominence.

Presently, the democratic system in operation in worldly nations is not according to Gandhian principles. We are not getting what Mahatma Gandhi ultimately cherished from democracy. If it is so, these nations could be devoid of atmosphere of non-violence and presence of fear. There could not have been corruption and divided human society. It is already emphasized that there could not have been problems pertaining to terrorism, communalism, regionalism and problems related to languages. More than this all, there could not have been observance of ethical and more degradation in public life. Such degradation is being observed constantly. The main cause after all these things remain that all activities of these nations are not non-violent. There cannot be any possibility of violence while there is gandhism in democracy. Mahatma Gandhi has once said that, 'Democracy and violence can never be mutual'.

Modern system of Government and Gandhian Peace:

The question arises before us as to how to guide modern system of government, especially democracy, towards Gandhian way, which undoubtedly has non-violence as its basic root. Then, it is to be made and quotable towards equal development of all citizens. This democracy must be such that "it should not warrant power of punishment". He was not against reason or rationality at all but his was a critique of the domineering and hegemonic nature of modern instrumental rationality. This modern hegemonic rationality has captured different aspects of modern life-style and Gandhi tried to criticise each of these one by one.

Modern machines and the kind of the functions these machines perform have developed another problematic feature of modern society, that is, universalism. Universalism is a trend where all people are thinking in a similar direction. All are living a similar kind of lifestyle and they cannot keep their individuality, their uniqueness alive as it will not be welcomed. Universalism not only kills an individual's initiative to do something new in a different manner, but it also enhances the tendency of centralisation and hegemony. And modern bureaucratic structures and political institutions like Parliament and State are some of the means which zealously try to be universal. For Gandhi, universalism is a violent philosophy perpetuated by the capitalists across the globe.

Gandhi was against any form of centralised tendency or universalism. He raised his voice for Swaraj and swadeshi. For Gandhi, the highly centralised and bureaucratic modern state represents violence in a concentrated and organised form. The individual has a soul, but as the state is a soulless machine, it can never be weaned away from violence to which it owns its very existence. Accordingly, modern states are structured in such a way that they encourage exploitation and violence discouraging the importance of the individual and his/ her local recognitions. That is why Gandhi used to say that the state dehumanised its citizens in more or less the same way as the medical, legal and other modern institutions. It had a vested institutional interest in monopolising all initiative and fostering a state-centered political culture. The more its citizens became 'addicted' to it and the more they felt helpless without it, the safer it felt. Accordingly, it systematically nurtured the illusion that the problems of society were too complex and intractable to be solved by ordinary citizens acting individually or collectively, and was best left to the state and its official agencies. It felt threatened by active and independent-minded citizens determined to participate in the conduct of their affairs and worried lest they should be morally compromised by what it did in their name. It therefore, denied them access to vital information and opportunities for political participation, and discouraged independent and vibrant local communities capable of challenging its decision.

A well-known Gandhian philosopher, Gopinath Dhawan, writes in this context that Gandhi sincerely believed that the state represented an organisation based on force. It manifested its coercive power through compulsion and exploitation of individuals in society. Gandhi decried any action of individuals in the state which was immoral, since in his scheme of thinking every action was judged by the touchstone of ethical priority. He argued that "no action which is not voluntary can be called moral...if we want to call an action moral, it should have been done consciously and as a matter of duty".

Gandhi wanted to persuade the politicians to accept the institution of state and power not as an end in itself but as an instrument. Accordingly, the state shall be regarded as a servant of the society and all its deeds should be guided by the sense of duty. Gandhi looked upon an increase in the power of the state with the greatest fear, because although while apparently doing well by minimising exploitation, it does the greatest harm to mankind destroying individuality, which lies at the root of all progress.

Destroying individuality means exploitation leading to violence. Therefore, to avoid violence and to ensure maximum flowering of the human personality, decentralisation of political power must become an end of a progressive and welfare-oriented society. For Gandhi, politics should be treated only as means. The state should try to decentralise its power. As much power a state will disperse, that much non-violent it will become. According to Gandhi, rights are not to be claimed but these are a kind of social value through which the individual will move on to the path of self-realisation. And in Gandhi's account, if an individual is embedded with moral and human values, then automatically s/he will achieve rights to actualise his/her humanitarian deeds. Then the importance of the institution of the state as a law providing institution would automatically wither away. There is then a state of enlightened anarchy. In such a state sovereignty vests in everyone who is his own ruler. He governs himself in a manner that he represents the freedom of his neighbours and in all such activity there is no political power because there is no state. But a single trait of all these features is not found in the modern state.

In Ramrajya there is not any notion of state at all. Swaraj, the second best option, is to be obtained by educating the masses to a sense of their capacity to regulate and control authority. This Swaraj would be of each and every individual, whosoever is residing there inside the state by accepting the importance of differences of caste, community, society and the different cultural and historical backgrounds. Because these are some factors through which an individual gets his/her recognition. Thus, Gandhi criticised the universalistic tendency of modernism. As per Ronald J. Terchek, Gandhi sees the universalising impulse of modernity as inhospitable of plurality. In its search for general rules, modern reason seeks to identify relevant verities and discards superfluous one what remains outside of the realm of the verifiable is unimportant to the enterprise replicated with the same result by distant, neutral strangers.

Conclusion:

Polity must be fearless, full of equality, providing protection to all eternal values and only then it can be pro-people. Gandhian principle of non-violence is very much significant in modern system of government from this point of view. This significance is likely to be of permanent nature perpetually.

Chapter-12

Mahatma Gandhi's View on Socialism and Communism

Socialism stood as an opposition to Capitalism. *Karl Marx* influenced *socialism* like no other and explained the economic structure and dictatorship of bourgeoisie through it. Marxism is a school based on Marx's idea which regarded socialism as a transition stage to communism.

Socialism is a political and economic theory of social organization which advocates that the means of production, distribution, and exchange should be owned or regulated by the community as a whole.

Socialism is a range of economic and social systems characterised by social ownership of the means of production and workers' self-management, as well as the political theories and movements associated with them. Social ownership can be public, collective or cooperative ownership, or citizen ownership of equity. There are many varieties of socialism and there is no single definition encapsulating all of them, with social ownership being the common element shared by its various forms.

Socialism in simple terms means 'theory or ideas that are social, economic, political that aim at making the society equal for all, and this theory advocates that the resources are used equally by the community as a whole'. When one talks of the socialism propounded by Gandhi, he/she is talking about the ideas of equality and equal sharing that Gandhi gave and which were used afterwards to initiate a new theory altogether- Gandhian Socialism. Gandhi never gave an exact framework to Gandhian Socialism, it was only after his death that intellects, educationists, thinkers mixed his thoughts and interpreted them into a new theory. (Hemlata Pandey, Journalist Jul 26, 2016)

The simple ideas related to socialism by Gandhi were like-

1. The idea of removing untouchability, as it was a barrier in bringing every community together. Gandhi wanted people to treat the so called 'lower castes' as equals and not mark any one as untouchable. The best thing was that Gandhi wanted the Harijans to stop thinking of them as of 'lower birth', because after all the suppression many people themselves had this mindset that they were not equal.
2. Gandhi supported the idea of self sustaining villages. He said that villages must get everyone together and work towards crop production, little businesses, etc, and share the resources equally. He believed that as villages were the smallest entities, it would be easier to popularise the idea of resource sharing. This resource sharing an idea of socialism.
3. The idea of class cooperation was supported by Gandhi. He asked people not to go for class struggle as it won't lead them anywhere; fighting for every resource would be of no use. But class cooperation would create a unified picture and with each other's assistance every class would be able to benefit equally.

4. He wanted people to go for intensive internal development. It is only when an individual understands his / her inner self that he/she is capable of contributing to the society.

Gandhian socialism is the branch of socialism based on the nationalist interpretation of the theories of Mahatma Gandhi. Gandhian socialism generally centres on Hind Swaraj or Indian Home Rule authored by Gandhi.

Gandhi was also never in favour of socialism propounded by Nehru, which emphasized on large-scale production. This massive production, Gandhi feared, would lead to greater exploitation and urbanization. It is this emphasis on decentralization that endeared Gandhi to Vinoba Bhave and Jayaprakash Narayan, and not to industrialists. According to Gandhi, for a real Swaraj to be established, it is not that one class rule be substituted by the other. It is much more than that.

The villages have to be strengthened. He further believed that is much easier to change an institution than a man. Though Gandhi had great faith in institutions and their functioning, he had greater faith in the perfectibility of the individual. Gandhi strongly believed that Western socialism and communism had a strong sense of selfishness.

He wanted the capitalists and the landlords act as trustees holding their wealth for the good of their villages, workers and the peasants. His theory of trusteeship wherein the economically powerful people would surrender their power voluntarily was severely criticized. Scholars like M. N. Roy stated that such a theory would benefit only the propertied class and that the exploited could win their rights only through violence and expropriation.

However, Gandhi opined that violence might destroy one or two bad rulers, two capitalists but such capitalists always crop up. So, the only solution, according to Gandhi, was to change men and not destroy them. Further, Gandhi stated that rich cannot accumulate wealth without the cooperation of the poor; and therefore, if the poor does not cooperate with the rich they naturally mend their ways.

Gandhi also gave his own definition to the word socialism. According to Gandhi, it does not refer to nationalization of the means of production, distribution, exchange, but faith in God, truth, non-violence and equality. So, in simple terms, Gandhian socialism is based on the ideas of non-possession and trusteeship.

It was thus not an ideology of industrialization, planning or state action and, therefore, it does not appeal to the intelligentsia. Further, Gandhian socialism was humanitarian in nature. It cared for the poor and it was a moral code of personal conduct than an economic ideology. It did not envisage the expropriation of the rich through violence or state action.

Gandhi's concept of socialism is different than Marxism socialism (Ben Thompson, Jul 26, 2018). Marxism is an economic principle, in simple terms it's the redistribution of wealth. Marxist theory attempts to break down value based on goods, labor, and the cost of production. In a capitalist system if you do well, you're rewarded. In a Marxist / Socialist system you're paid for the job you do, no matter how well you do it. So if you work your ass off, you make the same as the guy who just shows up.

This is also the problem with equality of outcome. Equality of outcome essentially means that everyone is equally compensated, as explained; it simply doesn't work in practice. If everyone gets treated equally, then where's the motivation to excel, or to apply yourself? If the guy next to you who's barely working gets paid as much as you no matter how hard you work, eventually you reach the point of realizing that it's pointless. Then you end up with a society where no one applies themselves because there's no real point.

This is why there is no Socialist country leading in any Tech sector, Industrial sector, or anything, except for maybe agricultural output, and the only reason for that would be because of the over reliance on manpower for production. In fact most socialist countries end up with food shortages.....

Gandhi's concept was more of a commune where everyone shared responsibility for general tasks, taking turns doing the things required to function. For instance cleaning latrines, or tending to animals.

The reason this was done is because India had a class system. The lowest were called "untouchables" they did the dirtiest of jobs, garbage collection, sewer work, etc... They were basically treated as worthless people, invisible to everyone else. Gandhi created his commune out of protest of this system, and demanded that everyone participate in even the tasks that were viewed as done only by untouchables.

Gandhi's view on Communism:

Communism is defined as a system where all property is public and people work and is given things by the government according to their needs.

Communism means a theory or system of social organization in which all property is owned by the community and each person contributes and receives according to their ability and needs.

Socialism is at its core an economic philosophy, whereas Communism is economic and political in its requirement that government be the central owner and decision maker in all matters. Communism rejects any religion and in a true Communist state religion is effectively abolished.

As far as Gandhi's ideas on Communism are concerned, though he appreciated its ability to organize masses, he was disappointed that it leads to the establishment of dictatorship. For a Gandhian, an alternative to communism is to establish a society wherein the instruments of production are simple and that the common man could play them in the villages.

In such a society, there would be no concentration of economic power, and so state would wither away and the Marxian dream would not be fulfilled. However, thinkers like M. N. Roy strongly criticized the ideas expressed by Gandhi and stated that he regretted that Gandhi taught his workers not to look upon their employers as exploiters but trust them as their elder brothers and that landlords were happy that Gandhi regarded them as trustees of the interests of the peasants.

He criticized Gandhi for his weak and watery reformism. Gandhi was further criticized for not having a progressive economic ideology that could give him a proper lead to the masses. In short. Communists countered any activity undertaken by Gandhi owing to their reservations against the economic and social philosophy of Gandhi. This antagonism was reflected in their denial to support Gandhi's Quit India movement, despite their criticism of Gandhian philosophy.

Communists had great regards for Gandhi as a great humanist. Commenting on Gandhi's idealism, E. M. S. Namboodiripad in one of his books 'The Mahatma and The Ism' stated that moral values like truth, non-violence, renunciation of the pleasures of life, political ideals like freedom, democracy, emancipation of women, unity of all religious groups and communities, etc., were ail indivisible parts of his life and teachings. But, unfortunately, Gandhi regarded the workers and peasants as brothers and partners of the classes that oppressed them.

Advocacy for Socialism & Communism:

Gandhi was an advocate for socialism and communism, but warned that it was not the same as that imagined by the Europeans and Americans. Writing in the English Daily Amrita Bazar Patrika on August 2-3, 1934, he said, "Socialism and communism of the West are based on certain conceptions which are fundamentally different from ours. One such conception is their belief in essential selfishness of human nature. I do not subscribe to it for I know that the former can respond to the call of the spirit in him, can rise superior to the passions that he owns in common with the brute and, therefore, superior to selfishness and violence, which belong to the brute nature and not to the immortal spirit of man ... Our socialism or communism should, therefore, be based on nonviolence and on harmonious co-operation of labour and capital, landlord and tenant."

Gandhi categorically rejected class war as being incompatible with nonviolence: "The idea of class war does not appeal to me. In India a class war is not inevitable, but it is avoidable if we have understood the message of nonviolence. Those who talk about class war as being inevitable have not understood the implications of nonviolence or have understood them only skin-deep."

He believed that communism could be built without abolishing the class-structure of society. He thought it possible to convince capitalist and worker to cooperate instead of being in conflict: "I am working for the co-operation and co-ordination of capital and labour, of landlord and tenant ... I have always told mill owners that they are not exclusive owners of mills and workmen are equal sharers in ownership. In the same way, I would tell you that ownership of your land belongs as much to the riots as to you, and you may not squander your gains in luxurious or extravagant living, but must use them for the well-being of riots. Once you make your riots experience a sense of kinship with you and a sense of security that their interests as members of a family will never suffer at your hands, you may be sure that there cannot be a clash between you and them and no class war."

At the same time Gandhi believed in struggling against exploitation: "I never said that there should be co-operation between the exploiter and the exploited so long as exploitation and the will to exploit persist. Only I do not believe that the capitalists and the landlords are all exploiters by an inherent necessity or that there is a basic or irreconcilable antagonism between their interests and those of the masses. All exploitation is based on co-operation, willing or forced, of the exploited. However much we may detest admitting it, the fact remains that there would be no exploitation if people refuse to obey the exploiter." For Gandhi struggle should be conducted through nonviolence, and he warned that one must never be passive in the face of evil; that violence was better than cowardice.

Gandhi foresaw a socialist India achieved through nonviolence. As he wrote in Harijan in 1940 (quoted in My View of Trusteeship), "Antagonism between the classes will be removed. I do not envisage a dead and artificial level among the people. There will be a variety among them as there is among the leaves of a tree. There will certainly be no have-nots, no unemployment, and no disparity between classes and masses such as we see to-day. I have no doubt whatsoever that if non-violence in its full measure becomes the policy of the State, we shall reach essential equality without strife."

Gandhi's analysis was paradoxical. On the one hand he rejected class struggle and foresaw cooperation between the classes. On the other hand, he called for perpetual struggle against exploitation and foresaw the day when there would be no more social classes. In the end it would seem that his strategic vision was a classless society not unlike that foreseen in the Communist Manifesto but that the means for arriving there was through nonviolence rather than violence.

Comparative ideologies of Communism

Bolshevism is the necessary result of modern materialistic civilization. Its insensate worship of matter has given rise to a school which has been brought up to look upon material advancement as the goal and which has all touch with the final things life.

[The collected Works of Mahatma Gandhi, Vol. XV, p. 168]

I am yet ignorant of what exactly Bolshevism is. I have not been able to study it. I do not know whether it is for the good of Russia in the long run. But I do know that in so far as it is based on violence and denial of God, it repels me. I do not believe in short-violent-cuts to success. Those Bolshevik friends who are bestowing their attention on me should realize that, however much I may sympathize with and admire worthy motives, I am an uncompromising opponent of violent methods even to serve the noblest of causes.

[Young India, 11-12-24, p. 406]

What does Communism mean in the last analysis? It means a classless society-an ideal that is worth striving for. Only I part company with it when force is called to aid for achieving it.... The idea of inequality, of "high or low" is an evil, but I do not believe in eradicating evil from the human breast at the point of the bayonet.

[Harijan, 13-3-37, p. 40]

"What do you think of Communism? Do you think it would be good for India?"

Communism of the Russian type, that is Communism which is imposed on a people, would be repugnant to India. I believe in non-violent communism...

"But Communism in Russia is against private property. Do you want private property?"

If communism came without any violence, it would be welcome. For then no property would be held by anybody expect on behalf of the people and for the people. A millionaire may have his millions, but he will hold them for the people. The State could take charge of them whenever they would need them for the common cause.

"Is there any difference of opinion between you and Jawaharlal in respect of Socialism?"

There is, but it is a difference in emphasis. He perhaps puts an emphasis on the result, whereas I put on the means. Perhaps according to him I am putting an over-emphasis on non-violence, would want to have Socialism by other means, If it was impossible to have it by non-violence. Of course my emphasis on non-violence becomes one of principle. Even If I was assured that we could have independence by means of violence, I should refuse to have it. It won't be real independence.

[Harijan, 13-2-37, p. 6]

I must confess that I have not yet been able fully to understand the meaning of Bolshevism. All that I know is that it aims at the abolition of the institution of private property. This is the only an application of the ethical ideal of non-possession in the realm of economics and if the people adopted this ideal of their own accord or could be made to accept it by means of peaceful persuasion, there would be nothing like it. But from what I know of Bolshevism it not only does not preclude the use of force but freely sanctions it for the expropriation of private property and maintaining the collective State of ownership of the same. And if that is so, I have no hesitation in saying that the Bolshevik regime in its present form cannot last for long. For it is my firm conviction that nothing enduring can be built on violence. But be that as it may there is no questioning the fact that the Bolshevik ideal has behind it the purest sacrifice of countless men and women who have given up their all for its sake, and an ideal that is sanctified by the sacrifices of such master spirits as Lenin cannot go in vain: the noble example of their renunciation will be emblazoned forever and quicken and purify the ideal as time passes.

[Young India, 15-11-28, p. 381]

I have made the workingmen's cause my own long before any of the young Communists here were born. I spent the best part of my time in South Africa working for them, I used to live with them, and shared their joys and sorrows. You must therefore understand why I claim to speak for labour. I expect at least courtesy from you if nothing else. I invite you to come to me and discuss things with me as frankly as you can.

You claim to be Communists, but you do not seem to live the life of Communism. I may tell you that I am trying my best to live up to the ideal of Communism in the best sense of the term. And Communism does not, I fancy, exclude courtesy. I am amongst you today, within a few minutes I will leave you. But if you want to carry the country with you, you ought to be able to react on it by reasoning with it. You cannot do so by coercion. You may deal destruction to bring the country round to your view. But how many will you destroy? Not tens of millions. You may kill a few thousands if you had millions with you. But today you are no more than a handful. I ask you to convert the Congress if you can and to take charge of it. But you cannot do so by bidding goodbye to the elementary rules of courtesy. And there is no reason why you should be lacking in ordinary courtesy, when it is open to you to give the fullest vent to your views, when India is tolerant enough to listen patiently to anyone who can talk coherently.

[Young India, 26-3-31, p. 53]

The Communists seem to have made troubleshooting their profession. I have friends among them. Some of them are like sons to me. But it seems they do not make any distinction between fair and foul, truth and falsehood. They deny the charge. But their reported acts to sustain it. Moreover, they seem to take their instructions from Russia, whom they regard as their spiritual home rather than India. I cannot countenance this dependence on an outside power. I have even said that we should not depend even on Russian wheat in our present food crisis. We must have the ability and courage to subsist on what our soil can give us rather than on foreign charity. Otherwise, we shall not deserve to exist as an independent country. The same applies to foreign ideologies country. The same applies to foreign ideologies. I would accept them only to the extent that I can assimilate them and adapt them to the Indian scene. But I must refuse to go under them.

My formula for the Communists, therefore, is that I would prefer to die at their hands, but I will not retaliate.

[Harijan, 6-10-46, pp. 338-39]

❍ ❍ ❍

Chapter-13

Gandhi and Development

Philosophy:

Gandhi envisioned a new social order based on his principles, where the economic development is coupled with moral progress and philanthropy. His philosophy of economic and social development visualizes a village as a self-sufficient unit which achieves development through means that are just, non-violent and ethical.

Idea:

Gandhi's basic aim was to have an all-round development of the society that included human development along with socio-economic, political development. Gandhian programme is holistic and multidimensional. The objective of his constructive work is the creation of non-violent society

Approach:

Theoretically, Gandhian approach to rural development may be labelled as 'idealist'. It attaches supreme importance to moral values and gives primacy to moral values over material conditions.

Gandhian Concept of Development:

1. Overview:

1. It attaches importance to the generation of maximum

possible employment opportunities in rural areas, especially for the weaker section of the community so as to enable them to improve their standard of living. Gandhian approach to rural development may be labelled as "Idealistic" as it attaches supreme importance to moral values and give preference to moral values over material conditions. The concept of 'Ram Rajya' is the basis of Gandhi's idea of an ideal social order. Gandhi defined Ram Rajya as "sovereignty of the people based on moral authority". In the Gandhian scheme, 'Rama' stood for God or one's 'inner voice'; Gandhi believed is a democratic social order in which people are supreme. Their supremacy is, however, not absolute. It is subject

2. Ideal Village: The village is the basic unit of the Gandhian ideal social order. Gandhi concisely pointed out, "If the village perishes India will perish too.... We have to make a choice between India of the village that is as ancient herself and India of the cities which are a creation of foreign domination". Gandhi's ideal village belongs to the Pre-British period, when Indian village were supposed to constitute voluntary federation of self-governing autonomous republic, and the work of Central Authority was to coordinate, supervise and manage village republics. The Central Authority will have no power to enforce its decision on village republics except the moral pressure or power of persuasion.

2. Decentralization:

1. Gandhi firmly believes that village republics can

be built only through decentralisation of social and political power. In such a system decision-making power will be vested in the Village Panchayat rather than in the State and the national capital. The representatives would be elected by all adults for a fixed period of five years. The elected representatives would constitute a council, called the Panchayat.

2. Resources for Gandhian Approach to managing village affairs would be raised from the villages. All the conflicts and disputes would be resolved within the village.
3. Apart from managing its own affairs the village would also be capable of defending itself against any invasion. A non-violent peace bridge of volunteers would be organized to defend the village. This corps would be different from the usual military formation. They would response the utmost faith in no-violence.

3. Self Sufficiency:

1. The village should be self-sufficient as for as its basic needs- food, clothing and other necessities are concerned. The village has to import certain things which it cannot produce in the village.
2. Village economy should be planned with a view to providing full employment to all the adult of the village. Each man should be guaranteed employment to enable him to meet his basic needs in the village itself so that he is not forced to migrate to town.
3. Gandhi focused on physical labour and said, "If all laboured for their bread than there would be enough

food and enough leisure for all". Shriman Narayan rightly observed, "Gandhi recognized toil to be not a curse but the joyful business of life as it has power to make man healthier, merrier, fitter and kindlier".

4. Industrialization:

1. Gandhi maintained that industrialization would help only a few and will lead to concentration of economic power. Industrialization leads to passive or active exploitation of the village. It encourages competition. Large scale production requires marketing. Marketing means profit-seeking through an exploitative mechanism. Moreover, industrialization replaces manpower and hence it a adds to unemployment but force labourers to migrate to urban areas. This will ruin village.
2. In order to avoid such a catastrophe, village and cottage industries should be revived . They provide employment to meet the needs of the villagers and facilitate village self-sufficiency. Gandhians are not against machine, if only it meets two aims: self sufficiency and full employment. According to Gandhi, there would be no objection to villagers.

5. Trusteeship:

1. Gandhi emphasized the principal of trusteeship in social and economic affairs. He firmly believed that all social property should be held in trust. The capitalists would take care not only of themselves but also of others. Some of their surplus wealth would be used for the rest of the society.

2. The poor workers, under trusteeship, would consider the capitalists as their benefactor; and would response faith in their noble intentions. Gandhi felt that if such a trusteeship were established, the welfare of the workers would increase and the clash between the workers and employers would be avoided.
3. Gandhi firmly believed that land should not be owned by any individual. Land belongs to God. Hence, individual ownership of land should be shunned. For that a landowner should be persuaded to become a trustee of his land. Land belongs to the community and must be used for the welfare of the community. They are merely trustee. By persuasion the heart of landowner should be changed and they should be induced to donate their
4. In nutshell, Gandhi's concept of development is oriented to upliftment of common people. His approach to rural development strives to reconstruct village republics which would be non-violent, self-governed and self-sufficient so far as the basic necessities of village dwellers are concerned. Apart from creating a new socio-economic order, it Endeavour's to transform man; otherwise the changes in the socio-economic order will be short-lived.

Gandhian perspective of Development:

Thinking on Gandhi's perspective of development, we realize that his ideas are of crucial importance. His life remained 'experiments with Truth' and his concerns embraced the whole of human race and not just India, South Africa and England. His principles, evolved during his life span 1869 to 1948, cover not just the last part of the nineteenth century and the first half of the twentieth century, but rather transcend any time-frame. The world has changed dramatically since he lived and worked. There have been enormous changes in political, economic and social scenes. However, trials, tribulations, and challenges faced by Mahatma in his eventful life remain important. The moral issues he raised are still relevant; and the questions he posed for social, economic, and political justice still remain of crucial importance. The prevalent methods of measuring development in terms of economic progress, industrialization, consumption of energy and urbanization have proved to be inadequate to address the issue of the miseries of the millions. Gandhi was aware of the pitfalls of such a theory and the results of the unequal distribution of wealth between different classes in a society. Today science and technology have taken unprecedented strides, and yet millions live in utter poverty; basic human rights are denied to them, powerful nations dominate over the powerless ones and innocent people become victims of terrorism. It is in this dismal situation that Gandhian perspective becomes useful. The quintessence of Gandhian philosophy is that the human values and not the market should govern life. Service of the teeming millions, the poor as " *Daridranarayan* - is of the utmost importance. Gandhi presents the' humane face of development. Ghosh brings out the following basic objectives of the Gandhian scheme of holistic development-

1. Human development (including moral development) for capability expansion,
2. development in a balanced way through manual and

intellectual labour (development of body, mind and soul),

3. development with social justice, rights and freedom. This is in accordance with the principle of social and human development.
4. attainment of self-sufficiency and self-reliance through rural development,
5. reduction in poverty through the generation of additional income and employment. (Ghosh, 2007: 213) Gandhi aims at what we may call sustainable development, balanced development of body, mind and soul. Gandhi had realized that human development is not just material or economic; it has to be moral, it should be able to instill the values of equality, liberty and dignity in the people; it must provide the persons with courage to protest against injustice. His emphasis on decentralization, community based economics; self-sufficiency, handicrafts, rural development, and use of low capital intensive appropriate technology indicate his vision for a self-sufficient economy.

According to Gandhi nature provides just enough, and not more, for our daily needs. He opposes exploitation, ruthless drive for economic abundance and personal aggrandizement, massive technological progress, severe competitions, unbridled consumerism and concentration of wealth and power. In his opinion, greed is detrimental to social good and political emancipation without economic equality is hollow. For him economics stands for social justice. (*Harijan,* October 9, 1937) He emphasizes decentralized self- dependent units bound together by the bonds of mutual cooperation and interdependence. For him the development of the individual and the development of the society are intertwined. His ultimate goal was *sarvodaya* (the development of all in all facets of life). The concept of *Sarvodaya* presupposes the principle of justice. *Sarvodaya* generates movements for changes, outward as well as inward and strives for egalitarian social order based on truth, nonviolence and purity of means. Gandhi never compromised at the cost of individual freedom, equality and social justice; his principle of nonviolence was not a mere philosophical principle but it was the rule of life. He had visualized an India where "all interests not in conflict with the interests of the dumb millions will be scrupulously respected, whether indigenous or foreign." (*Young India;* September10, 1931). Gandhi's basic aim was to have an all-round development of the society that included human development along with socio-economic- political development. Gandhian programme is holistic and multidimensional. The objective of his constructive work is the creation of non-violent society. Gandhi envisages a healthy society based on harmony and dialogue, where the ideas of equality and justice are translated in the lives of teeming millions. Commenting on man's social nature, Gandhi writes/' If it is his privilege to be independent it is equally his duty to be independent...It will be possible to reconstruct our villages so that villages collectively, not villagers individually, will become self-contained." (*Young Indi:* April 25, 1929). Gandhi believes in the unity of life and egalitarian values in all spheres of life. According to him life cannot be divided in sphere like social, political, economic, moral and religious. If one part of the society suffers, all parts suffer. We get an important insight from J. B. Kripalani and Dada Dharmadhikari. (Thakkar & Mehta, 2011). J. B. Kriplani points out that it is not unusual to have saints among us - saints who meditate for salvation and who are concerned with the uplift of the soul. It is their contribution to the evolution to the human history in an indirect way. But Gandhi was concerned in a direct way. Social involvement is very important to him. Gandhi visualized a society of diverse people based on mutual understanding, mutual cooperation and mutual respect. He wanted freedom and equality for all. Gandhi transcends barriers of religion, rituals, caste, class and colour. Dada Dharmadhikari points out that Gandhi had 'no business other than life, an integrated life'. He never ran away from any situation, he faced it. His concept of life was all comprehensive; for him nothing was separate and everything was harmonized. He added social dimension to morality that was unique. He practiced what he preached and did everything possible to identify himself with the common man, ordinary man, suffering man. When India became independent, he was not in the capital to celebrate, but was with the riot-stricken people. Gandhi maintains that wealth is to be used judiciously, governed by the principle of 'each according to his need'; and emergence of inequality has to be curbed at all levels. According to him, all amassing or hoarding of wealth, above and beyond one's legitimate requirement is theft. (*Harijan;* August 11, 1946). His concept of social use of wealth against the prevailing ethos of consumerism demands our serious attention. Values of 'truth' 'non-violence' and 'non-accumulation of wealth' are to be cherished for the very survival of the society, where the weakest has the same rights as the strongest. Trusteeship for Gandhi is a dynamic concept that can bring change in the established institutions. It is a means of transforming the present capitalist order of society into an egalitarian one. An individual is not free to hold or use his wealth for selfish satisfaction. (*Harijan*, October 25, 1952) .The common property is to be used for the good of one and all, all including the rich have to work for the society acc to his/her capacity and they will receive as per needs. Property owners are caretakers of the property for the common good. Trusteeship aims at some realizable outcomes like capital-labour cooperation, formation of social capital, reduction in concentration of economic power in a few hands, and voluntary cutting down the wants. Gandhi did not approve the use of machines that replaces men or makes them subservient to machines. He advocates judicious use of machines; and simple, indigenous technology of non-exploitative nature in tune with nonviolence. He emphasizes the importance of whatever can be produced locally, (From Yeravada Mandir, 1980:.44), and thinks about a decentralized economy. He propagated the use of the spinning wheel and *Khadi* for self reliance as well as moral and economic regeneration. Gandhi visualized exploitation free society, based on cooperation and ethics. His vision included productive employment for India's millions, schemes for rebuilding villages and creating communities of care and concern, promotion of *khadi* and local handicrafts, production of need-based basic goods, empowering people by imparting basic education and required skills to enable them to create decentralized structures of power, and ensuring equality of opportunity for all. He believed that human wants have to be limited, and no one should suffer from deprivation and want of basic necessities. And for that the required means of production should be socially controlled. His emphasis is on collectivity and not on individual needs and greed. Wealth has to be created collectively and enjoyed collectively.

For Gandhi rebuilding villages, in accordance with the principles of self-sufficiency and decentralization, was very important. To quote him, "I would say that if the village perishes, India will perish *too." (Harijan,* August 29, 1936). The nearest approach to civilization based on nonviolence was the erstwhile village republic of India. *(Harijan;* January 13, 1940) . According to him, cities have so far exploited the villages, and that has resulted in the gap between villages and cities in education, culture, facilities, employment. Now a new partnership between cities and villages is needed. Gandhi insists on regulation of wants and use of the goods and material not imported, but made in one's own country. His concept of *Swadeshi,* a dynamic concept of self-reliance, is closely connected with *Swaraj,* political freedom. Another of his important concept is that of 'bread labour', that propagates that some amount of physical labour has to be done by every person every day. Physical labour is a great equalizing force, and the need for socially useful manual labour is obvious. Influenced by John Ruskin, Gandhi maintained that all works are of equal dignity. He also said that in the conflict situation between the capital and the labour, cooperation and amicable settlements are the way out and not violence. The rift between the rich and the poor is increasing in our times and the exploitation involved in the process of the amassing wealth is blatant. Gandhi was sure that too much emphasis on materialism leads to violence and unhappiness. He criticized the exploitative and materialistic Western civilization and believed that India cannot be a replica of that. Many western thinkers also have noticed trends of exploitation and dehumanization trends of industrialization. Gandhi's critique of the exploitative and dehumanizing modern western civilization is relevant today, as it makes us aware of the fact that economic progress devoid of moral elements will not ultimately help the people but will make internal divisions and dissensions more intense. Parekh suggests that Gandhi's critique was directed to modern, materialistic society rather than the Western culture in general. He argues that the modern society is built and maintained by massive violence, and relationships are characterized by struggle, mastery, subjugation, domination, victory and defeat. (Parekh,' 1995: 20-26).

Gandhi connects violence with unbridled greed and vehement desire for luxuries. He had strongly advised the people to give up selfishness and to take the minimum for the satisfaction of wants. He firmly believed that unless there is a complete transformation in our economy and our style of life, peace will elude us, however hard we may strive for it. His relentless struggle against inequality and poverty, exploitation and suppression has many lessons for contemporary times. It is important to realize that he is opposed to the concentration of power and the system that makes the individual subservient to the material. Gandhi draws our attention to the need to protect the environment and to guard against the abuse of natural resources. Our mindless destruction of natural wealth is alarming. Mighty projects, big dams, giant industries and other massive ventures raise questions about the quality of life affected by them. The quest for the mirage of material development often leads to the destruction of forests, ecological imbalances, scarcity of water, soil erosion, silting of rivers and desertification pose grave dangers to environment. Gandhi encourages us to rethink about our inadequate and risky development model putting too much stress on economic prosperity. He does not believe in survival of the fittest, but survival and good survival of all, not greatest good of all, but greatest good of all. His talisman is of great value: "Whenever you are in doubt, try the following expedient. Recall the face of the poorest and the most helpless man whom you have seen and ask yourself whether the step you contemplate is going to be of any use to him/" Today we need a more human-centric, moral-centric worldview and way of living, and Gandhi shows us that. Making opportunities available for all members in the society for their full development and having full civic engagement of the citizens are Gandhian principles that are of vital importance today. Commitment to the idea and practice of democracy blooms not in the houses of deliberation and debate. It starts at the level of one's own life. Self sufficiency at personal level and eagerness to perish for the higher cause are the basis of the idea of oceanic circles. Few can grasp the complex ground realities and dare to find a way in the labyrinth of ideologies and power games. Few have the clear understanding of the processes of governance and development coupled with empathy and sensitivity. And few have the openness for innovative thinking, strategies and ways of doing. Gandhi is one individual who dared to think and act differently to make the difference to the conflict-ridden society and power-hungry states. At this juncture we need to understand why Gandhi is so important for us. An important way is to understand the issues and challenges of our times in the context of Gandhi's ideas and life. During his visit to India in 1959, Martin Luther King was asked a question at a press conference "Where is Gandhi today? We see him nowhere." His reply was "Gandhi is inevitable. If humanity wants to progress, Gandhi is a must. We may ignore Gandhi at our own risk." This insight is of crucial importance to all of us in our times.

Gandhian Model of Development:

Gandhian model of development is based upon the following salient features:

1. Gandhian Model is totally different from Western materialistic model of development. It gives place of primacy to moral development and ethical view of socio-economic-political development. Truth and non-violence are advocated as the basis of all human activities and decisions.
2. It stands for complete decentralization of functions and powers with each village acting as a self-regulating and self-sufficient unit of development.
3. Development must ensure food, clothing, shelter, education and employment for all.
4. Strong reservation about mechanization and industrialisation. Machines deprive human beings of employment and industrialization generates consumerism and profiteering. Industrialization

must be based upon the use of manpower and its aim should be to meet the primary basic needs of all the people.

5. Emphasis upon cottage industries, handicrafts, agriculture and labour.
6. Total emphasis upon social equality, non-violence, truthful living, social responsibilities, dignity of labour and moral and spiritual happiness. Development has to be measured on the scale of happiness and not consumerism and profit-making.
7. All development must ensure environmental health and happiness.
8. Gandhian view of a developed state is a peaceful, happy, non-violent state based on morality and respect for the equal dignity, worth and needs of all the people of society. .

The critics of this model hold it to be an idealist model which cannot be really used. However, the supporters of the presently popular model of sustainable development appreciate the value of Gandhian Model of Development.

Chapter - 14

Gandhian Institutions "Sarvodaya"

Philosophy of 'Sarvodaya':

Mahatma Gandhi almost predicted in Hind Swaraj as he prepared its manuscript in 1908. Gandhi put forward four main goals before youth for humanity, so as to move towards its destiny. These were Swaraj, Non-violence, Swadeshi and Sarvodaya. Sarvodaya as one of the pillars to bring Hind Swaraj. Gandhian philosophy of Sarvodaya was for changing attitude of youth & aware them for their rights & duties.

Meaning of Sarvodaya:

Sarvodaya is a Sanskrit term; it means 'universal uplift' or 'progress of all'. That term was used by Mohandas K. Gandhi as the title of his 1908 translation of John Ruskin's tract on political economy, *"Unto This Last"*, and Gandhi came to use the term for the ideal of his own political philosophy. Later Gandhian, like the Indian nonviolence activist Vinoba Bhave, embraced the term as a name for the social movement in post-independence India which strove to ensure that self-determination and equality reached all strata of India society.

Inspiration for Sarvodaya:

Gandhi received a copy of Ruskin's "Unto This Last" from

a British friend, while working as a lawyer in South Africa in 1904. Going through that book he determined to change his life in accordance with the ideals of the book. Gandhi advances the concept of Sarvodaya, which were the based on three basic concepts :

- That the good of the individual is contained in the good of all.
- That a lawyer's work has the same value as the barber's in as much as all have the same right of earning their livelihood from their work.
- That is a life of labour, i.e., the life of the tiller of the soil and the handicraftsman is the life worth living.

Simple Living & High Thinking:

Mahatma Gandhi was of the firm view that the earth provides enough to satisfy every man's needs, but not for every man's greed. In the 'Sarvodaya' society of his dream, therefore, every member will be free from any greed for limitless acquisition of material wealth and more and more luxurious living and they will follow the motto of simple living and high thinking. Everyone will, thus, get ample opportunity to produce and earn sufficiently through honest work for decent and dignified living. Consequently there will be no problem of unemployment. Of course, obviously, income of different people may be different, depending on their talent, ability and effort. But those who will earn more will use the bulk of their greater earnings for the good of the society as a whole. In such a society, all wealth, including land, will be assumed as common property to be utilized for the welfare of all. If an individual has more than his proportionate portion, he becomes a trustee of the excess wealth for the benefit of the less fortunate members of the society. As regards use of machinery in economic activity, Gandhi said that "If we feel the need of machines, we certainly will have them. But there should be no place for machines which concentrate power in a few hands and turn the masses into mere machine-minders, if, indeed, they do not make them unemployed." In order, therefore, to minimize use of machines in a Sarvodaya society, Gandhi strongly advocated that everyone should do some productive physical work at least to earn his/her daily bread as was also advocated by Leo Tolstoy a "the great Russian thinker and writer and everyone should uphold the dignity of labour irrespective of the type of honest labour performed by an individual.

Objects of Sarvodaya Movement:

The Sarvodaya Movement has as its target the establishment of a whole network of such self-supporting village communities. The family relationships which are confined at present to the blood group will be extended to cover the whole village where distinctions based on race, creed, caste, language and so forth will completely be eliminated. Agriculture will be so planned that all the people will have enough to consume. Industry will be conducted on a cottage basis till all the people in the village are gainfully employed. The needs of the village will be determined by the people of the village themselves, through Village Council, representative of the whole village.

Sarvodaya Movement:

Gandhi's ideals have lasted well beyond the achievement

of one of his chief projects, Indian independence (Swaraj). His followers in India (notably, Vinoba Bhave) continued working to promote the kind of society that he envisioned, and their efforts have come to be known as the Sarvodaya Movement. Anima Bose has referred to the movement's philosophy as "a fuller and richer concept of people's democracy than any we have yet known." Sarvodaya workers associated with Vinoba, J. P. Narayan, Dada Dharmadhikari, Dhirendra Mazumdaar, Shankarrao Deo, K. G. Mashruwala undertook various projects aimed at encouraging popular self-organization during the 1950s and 1960s, including Bhoodan and Gramdan movements. Many groups descended from these networks continue to function locally in India today.

Principles of the Sarvodaya:

- There is no centralized authority, and there is political and economic atmosphere in the villages.
- Politics will not be the instrument of power but an agency of service and *Rajnity* will yield place to *Loknity*.
- All people will be imbued with the spirit of love, fraternity, truth, non-violence and self-sacrifices. Society will function on the basis on the non-violence.
- There will be no party system and majority rule and society will be free from the evil of the tyranny of the majority.
- The sarvodaya society is socialist in the true sense of the term. All calling will be the same moral, social and economical values. The individual personality has the fullest scope for development.

- The sarvodaya society is based on equality and liberty. There is no room in it for unwholesome some competition, exploitation and class-hatred.

Sarvodaya stands for the progress of the all. All individual should do individual labour and follow the ideal of non possession. Then it will be possible to realize the goal of: from each according

- to his work and to each according to his needs.
- There will be no private property, the instrument of exploitation and the source of social distinctions and hatred. Similarly, the profit motive will disappear, rent and interest to will go.
- The Sarvodaya Movement is based on Truth, Non-violence and Self-denial.
- The Sarvodaya Movement makes a sincere and bold attempt to create the necessary atmosphere to bring together such individuals with an unwavering faith in the Welfare of All
- The gain to the individual would be small. The development of each quality depends upon every other. If all the qualities are improved a little, then the individual would gain more.

Agency of Common Welfare:

Sarvodaya is an agency of Service for Common Welfare Sarvodaya sets its face squarely against the politics of power and exploitation. It lays great emphasis on moral and spiritual values. It seeks to create new social and economical values. The concept of possession yields place to the concept of trusteeship. People will work for the good of all and family feeling will animate the entire community. There will be fullest scope for freedom, fellowship and equality. The state is to be an agency of power. Gramrajya is a base of non-violence. Sarvodaya stands for good of all and not for the good of any particular individual or class. Bhoodan at the early stage, Gramdan at a later stage and Sampattidan will bring about a change of heart. The rich and poor will give up their ideas of attachment to private property and will strive to work for the good of all.

Conclusion:

So, lastly we can conclude that Sarvodaya ideals are not practicable. Though the ideals of sarvodaya will be noble. Nobady can find fault with them, in the actual world. They will be found wanting. It will be almost impossible to establish a society strictly on the basis of great principles by Mahatma Gandhi and others. Sarvodaya doctrines are soaring and it is doubtful whether they can rest on the earth. The poor record of Panchayat Raj in India bears testimony to the backward condition in which people are. In the highly competitive world, one country can not succeed in having Gramraj. Unless all states in the world accept the Sarvodaya idea. The chances of having it is a particular country like India are bleak. As well as, it is difficult to bring a change of the heart in the youth, who is given to selfishness. People donated useless land in response to the Bhoodan.

So, need of the present era for youth is 'Think Globally and Act Locally'.

Chapter-15

Mahatma Gandhi's vision adopted in Constitution of India

Gandhian Constitution for free India:

It was published in early 1946, which was drafted by Shriman Narayan Agrawal, on the basis of writings of Mahatma Gandhi. Constitution was 60 page document divided in 22 chapters that includes Basic Principles, Fundamental rights & duties, Provincial Government, central Government & Judiciary. It was mostly descriptive & explanatory in draft form. Though, the document contained noteworthy features with strong advocacy for decentralized politics & administrative setup with village Panchyat as core unit. Village Panchyat were given power that includes judicial function as well. Fundament duties were conjoined with fundamental rights. It contained a provision for "Right to bear arms" too.

Gandhian constitution was viewed as one of the efforts of Indians to put forward "Alternative Constitutional Imaginings". But it is not clear how Gandhian constitution were received by intellectual ambience.

After constitution was enacted in 1950, Gandhian Constitution was often cited in scholarly work that dealt alternative conception of democracy, decentralization & his thoughts.

Constitution of India:

Mahatma Gandhi was mass leader not a committee man. So he was not a member of Constituent Assembly. Yet there were many members in constituent assembly that followed his vision. Years ago, writings in his magazine YOUNG INDIA in 1931 and provision of his constitution were significantly discussed in the assembly. Thus, constitution of India while being drafted was modulated around Gandhi's thoughts about communal discrimination, women empowerment, and his envision of India as a country who followed equality, liberty and fraternity.

The constitution of India has been enacted to strengthen the Panchyat System in villages in a bid to strengthen democratic institution at grass root level. The underlying idea is to make Panchyata as vibrant unit of self government and local administration local level. (Article. 40)

Raising slandered of Living in Directive Principles of the constitution Article 47, obligates the state to regard, as among its primary duties, the raising of the level of nutrition and slandered of living of its people and the improvement of public health. In particular, the state to endeavor to bring about

Prohibition of the consumption, except for medicinal purposes, of intoxicating drinks (Alcohol etc.) and drugs which are injurious to health and promotion of cottage industry (Article 43)

❍❍❍

Chapter-16

Mahatma Gandhi's ideologies in India's Foreign Policy

Indian foreign policy of Non- alignment is based on Mahatma Gandhi's creed of non-violence. Gandhi consistently preached non-violence as an instrument for shaping the destinies of nations. Ahimsa (Non-violence) was his basic law for human conducts, which heals and restore men's nature, social order and justice. Gandhi firmly believed that non-violence is the best method to settle International disputes.

Non-violence in international politics:

In all annals of human history, it was the Mahatma Gandhi who used the principle of Non-Violence for the political purpose-to win freedom from an *alien* rule for his country. This was his greatest contribution to the world as a whole.

Nehru learnt from Gandhi, the principle of non-violence is irrefutable, and that it demands an altogether new type of state. For Gandhi, we live in an inextricably interlinked cosmos in which any form of violence is ultimately self-destructive. For the cosmologically minded, then, politics serves just one purpose: to erase violence. Gandhi pursued this precept within the confines of the British Empire, but his disciple's ambitions were greater. Nehru sought to apply his guru's practices not only within India but also in the realm of international politics.

Nehru extended the idea of sovereignty far beyond the old idea of survival for survival's sake. The Nehru vision state sought to eliminate violence, placing the calculus for action beyond history understood either as a Golden Age to be recovered or as a series of humiliations to be avenged. Instead, action was to be calculated on the basis of present conditions, to eliminate violence now.

However, this ideal posed a significant challenge: how could India non-violently confront violence? The solution lay in Gandhi's concept of *satyagraha*. This might itself seem violent because it challenged authority. Crucially, however, the practitioner of *satyagraha* was less violent than their opponent, and directed most of their violence inwards. Nehru made this his approach to foreign policy, and, though his country was impoverished, he did not hesitate to put it into practice. This earliest application of *satyagraha* to international politics continues to shape India's military border policy.

Modi: In Gandhi's mould?

It seems that Gandhi is palpable in all that Modi does. He has unveiled statues of the Mahatma around the globe, paid rich tributes to him, and put into practice many Gandhian ideas such as the campaign to "Clean India". However, the true import of his ideas lies not in the realm of the explicit but at the level of the intellect, and is most obvious in the thinking behind India's foreign policy.

Modi's renewal of non-violence as a guiding principle in foreign policy is deeply significant. Its effects will cascade across the world, remaking the global system.

In practice, this means widening the definition of violence and seeking it out for eradication with greater confidence, both domestically and externally. Modi did precisely this when he spoke of India's shortage of toilets. In other words, the belief is that India's focus on the quotidian, if successful, will transform the country.

It would be an abdication of the principle of non-violence if India tolerated violence from abroad to reduce it at home.

Mainly, India's foreign policy is constructed around the principle of non-violence. If this has not always been apparent, it isn't because of any dissimulation on the part of India's politicians and diplomats. The greatest stumbling block is that India's actions are so often misread. India's identity was never concealed, even if observers were incapable of understanding what they saw. It is necessary, therefore, to reach a new understanding of India. But this will not happen through the assiduous collection of new facts and figures alone if they continue to be misinterpreted. So, We must adopt an entirely new analytical framework that can encompass Gandhi's mission and his abiding influence.

"Panch Sheel" in Indian foreign policy:

India has also adopted the principle of "*Panch sheel*" in her foreign policy. First time it was mentioned in joint statement issued by Prime Minister of India and china on 28 June, 1954. The five principals as stated in it were:

1. Mutual respect for each other's territorial integrity & sovereignty.

2. Non-aggression.
3. Non interference in each other's internal affairs.
4. Equality & mutual benefit.
5. Peaceful existence.

Dr. Rajendra Prasad, 1st President, had noted that 'Panch Sheel' was based on Buddha's massage.

Chapter 17

Gandhi's Views to the Nation on Different Ocassion

An eye for an eye only ends up making the whole world blind.

Mahatma Gandhi

We may never be strong enough to be entirely nonviolent in thought, word and deed. But we must keep nonviolence as our goal and make strong progress towards it.

Mahatma Gandhi

I am prepared to die, but there is no cause for which I am prepared to kill. The human voice can never reach the distance that is covered by the still small voice of conscience.

Mahatma Gandhi

Strength does not come from physical capacity. It comes from an indomitable will

Mahatma Gandhi

A coward is incapable of exhibiting love; it is the prerogative of the brave.

Mahatma Gandhi

A man is but the product of his thoughts what he thinks, he becomes.

Mahatma Gandhi

A nation's culture resides in the hearts and in the soul of its people.

Mahatma Gandhi

Anger and intolerance are the enemies of correct understanding.

Mahatma Gandhi

I am prepared to die, but there is no cause for which I am prepared to kill.

Mahatma Gandhi

A policy is a temporary creed liable to be changed, but while it holds good it has got to be pursued with apostolic zeal.

Mahatma Gandhi

A principle is the expression of perfection, and as imperfect beings like us cannot practise perfection, we devise every moment limits of its compromise in practice.

Mahatma Gandhi

A religion that takes no account of practical affairs and does not help to solve them is no religion.

Mahatma Gandhi

A 'No' uttered from the deepest conviction is better than a 'Yes' merely uttered to please, or worse, to avoid trouble.

Mahatma Gandhi

It has always been a mystery to me how men can feel themselves honoured by the humiliation of their fellow beings.

Mahatma Gandhi

A small body of determined spirits fired by an unquenchable faith in their mission can alter the course of history.

Mahatma Gandhi

A weak man is just by accident. A strong but non-violent man is unjust just by accident.

Mahatma Gandhi

Action expresses priorities.

Mahatma Gandhi

Action is no less necessary than thought to the instinctive tendencies of the human frame.

Mahatma Gandhi

Religion is a matter of the heart. No physical inconvenience can warrant abandonment of one's own religion.

Mahatma Gandhi

All compromise is based on give and take, but there can be no give and take on fundamentals. Any compromise on mere fundamentals is a surrender. For it is all give and no take.

Mahatma Gandhi

Rights that do not flow from duty well performed are not worth having.

Mahatma Gandhi

All the religions of the world, while they may differ in other respects, unitedly proclaim that nothing lives in this world but Truth.

Mahatma Gandhi

It is health that is real wealth and not pieces of gold and silver.

Mahatma Gandhi

Forgiveness is choosing to love. It is the first skill of self-giving love.

Mahatma Gandhi

Always aim at complete harmony of thought and word and deed. Always aim at purifying your thoughts and everything will be well.

Mahatma Gandhi

Among the many misdeeds of the British rule in India, history will look upon the act depriving a whole nation of arms as the blackest.

Mahatma Gandhi

An error does not become truth by reason of multiplied propagation, nor does truth become error because nobody sees it.

Mahatma Gandhi

An ounce of practice is worth more than tons of preaching.

Mahatma Gandhi

To give pleasure to a single heart by a single act is better than a thousand heads bowing in prayer.

Mahatma Gandhi

God has no religion.

Mahatma Gandhi

They cannot take away our self-respect if we do not give it to them.

Mahatma Gandhi

Man should forget his anger before he lies down to sleep.

Mahatma Gandhi

I like your Christ, I do not like your Christians. Your Christians are so unlike your Christ.

Mahatma Gandhi

We must become the change we want to see.

Mahatma Gandhi

A vow is a purely religious act which cannot be taken in a fit of passion. It can be taken only with a mind purified and composed and with God as witness.

Mahatma Gandhi

The weak can never forgive. Forgiveness is the attribute of the strong.

Mahatma Gandhi

A man who was completely innocent, offered himself as a sacrifice for the good of others, including his enemies, and became the ransom of the world. It was a perfect act.

Mahatma Gandhi

❍❍❍

Chapter-18

Last Day of life of the Mahatma Gandhi

[Venkita Kalyanam, personal secretary to Mahatma Gandhi, recounts Friday, January 30, 1948, moment-by-moment—the day when the Mahatma was shot. He was just behind Gandhi when Naturam Godse fired his shots.]

Mahatma Gandhi arrived in Delhi on Tuesday, 9 September 1947, from Calcutta. He was staying in Birla House at Albuquerque Road (now renamed Tees January Marg—30th January Road). A large carpeted room with an attached toilet was placed at his disposal for use by his entourage. This was an all-purpose room in the ground floor of the huge mansion. Gandhiji usually spent the whole day here attending to his correspondence, talking to people, spinning his charkha and taking his midday siesta. There was also a balcony, fully enclosed with glass doors, adjoining the room where he would sleep at nights on the carpeted floor, along with the rest of us.

Friday, 30 January 1948, dawned like any other day. Nobody ever knew what was going to happen in that evening. Gandhi ji got up as usual for the prayers at 3.30 and went about daily routine. Gandhiji roused his grand niece Abha to get up.

After his ablutions, Gandhiji came out of the toilet and squatted on the mattress. All people accompanied with sat before him. Gandhiji's day always commenced with prayer. He described prayer as the key of the morning and bolt of the evening. His prayers included recitations from the scriptures of all religions, particularly *Hindusim and Islam,* in order to stress the essential unity of all religions.

Gandhi ji closed his eyes in meditation. Abha was still asleep. He had noticed her absence. Prayer was held without Abha's participation. Immediately after the prayer Manu went to the kitchen to fetch Gandhiji's morning beverage—a glass of hot water mixed with a tablespoonful of honey and lime. When she handed him the marble tumbler of nectar, Gandhi ji told her in Gujarati, 'It appears my influence, even among my close companions, is waning. Prayer is like a broomstick meant to cleanse one's soul. Abha's failure to participate in the prayer pains me. You all are aware of the importance I attach to prayer. If you have the courage, you may, on my behalf convey my displeasure to her. If she is not willing to participate in the prayer she should take leave of me. This will be in our joint interest!' Meanwhile, Abha got up and started attending to her work. Gandhiji, did not, for reasons known to him, confront her directly. Kalyanam continued to sit by his side to receive his instructions for the day. He wanted kalyanam to make arrangements for his visit to 'Sevagram' for ten days from 2nd February. Kalyanam placed before him the typed draft of the new constitution for the Indian National Congress which Gandhi had dictated to him the previous day, suggesting its disbandment and reconstitution as a new body with greater emphasis on social service and rural uplift. Gandhi summoned my Pyarelalji and handed the draft to him with instructions to peruse it carefully and make any suggestions or corrections that he may consider necessary.

Do Not Wish to Live Long

Conditions in Delhi were far from normal those days. There had been communal disturbances owing to the large influx of Hindu refugees from Pakistan. Having gone through unpleasant experiences at the hands of Muslims in Pakistan, they wanted to take revenge on Muslims in Delhi. Delegations of Muslim and Hindu leaders called on him every day to discuss ways and means of restoring normalcy in the capital.

During those cold winter days, Gandhiji preferred to spend the day sitting on a charpoy in the open lawn, basking in the sun. His daily engagements were crowded. He could never be seen idle. When he had no appointments he would be busy writing letters and articles in Gujarati, Hindi and English. While Ministers and other VIPs visited him by prior appointment, Pandit Nehru, whenever he was in station, made it a point to call on Gandhiji, at about 9 am, on his way to office.

Among the prominent visitors who met Gandhiji at that day was Mrs. R.K. Nehru, who came in at 6:00 AM. She was scheduled to leave for USA in the afternoon. At her request Gandhiji gave her an autographed photograph with the message, 'As a representative of a poor nation, you should lead a simple and frugal life while you are there'.

Though Gandhiji was the master of nine languages but in those days he was very much interested to learn 'Bangla' language. Gandhiji slept at 10:30 AM and when he got up in the midday he went to bathroom without any support. Looking this 'Bahuban' said you are looking differently. In response Gandhiji repliedh " ***Ekla Chalo re, Ekla Chalo re***" ( ) .

At 2:00 PM, Margaret Bourke White, famous photographer of the Life magazine interviewed Gandhiji. In the course of her conversation, she asked him, "You have always stated that you would like to live up to 125. What gives you that hope?" Gandhiji surprised her by answering that he no longer entertained that hope. When questioned why, he replied, "Because of the terrible happenings in the world. I do not want to live in darkness".

Most of his time at Birla House was spent in writing letters, meeting visitors and prayers. Soon after she left, Prof N.R. Malkhani, Deputy High Commissioner in Pakistan, met Gandhiji with two others and told him of the sad plight of the Hindus of Sind. After hearing them patiently, Gandhi replied, "These things would not have happened had people listened to me. I say things, which do not go home, yet I go on saying what I believe to be true. I know that I am a 'back number'."

Bob Stimsom of the BBC, who had submitted some questions to Gandhiji, was to meet him after the prayers. He had already arrived and proceeded straight to the lawn where Gandhiji was to hold the prayer. Chief Minister U N Dhebar and Rasiklal Parekh from Kathiawar and the celebrated author Vincent Shean, who had some interviews with Gandhiji in the last few days, had also come without prior appointment in the hope of meeting Gandhiji. All of them were disappointed. Birla House had its own watchmen at the gate. There had been objections to the recitation of the Koran at Gandhiji's earlier public meetings in the previous year. Sardar Patel had therefore, in his capacity as Home Minister, ordered the deployment of one head constable and four foot-constables at Birla House as a precautionary measure.

Men Who Want Security Have No Right To Live:

Gandhiji would have none of it and told him bluntly that his life was in the hands of God and that if he had to die no precautions could save him. 'Those who preferred security to freedom had no right to live', he said. He would rather stop holding public prayer meetings than agree to any such personal search. Police in plain clothes were then asked to keep a watch on suspicious characters and prevent anyone from attacking Gandhiji while he was on his way to the prayer and back. At two in the afternoon Abha and Manu had, with Gandhiji's permission, gone to visit some friends, promising to return in time for the evening prayers. The responsibility of serving Gandhiji's evening meal fell on kalyanum. Although the government had been in office for only five months, the media was full of alleged differences between Pandit Nehru and Sardar Patel. Gandhiji was distressed with these rumours and wanted to counter this. He was even thinking of asking Sardar Patel to resign so that Nehru may have a free hand to conduct the affairs of the country. But that didn't happen. He had summoned Patel for a discussion at 4 pm and intended to speak on the subject after the prayers, but that was not to be. Accompanied by his daughter Maniban, Patel arrived on time when Gandhiji was having his frugal supper. While they were conversing, Abha and Manu had also arrived.

The Last Meeting with Sardar Ballabhbai Patel:

Prayer was scheduled to start at 5 pm. The discussion between Gandhiji and Patel continued beyond 5 pm. In view of the importance and seriousness of the talk about the differences of Nehru & Patel, none of who were there dared to disturb them. Ultimately the talk ended . After that, Gandhi went to the toilet and immediately proceeded to the prayer ground in Birla House, which was nearly 30-40 yards away. There were four or five steps and then there was a big lawn. Gandhiji was late by fifteen minutes for the prayer meeting. There were about 250 people anxiously awaiting his arrival. Gandhiji walked briskly as usual with his head bent and his glance glued to the ground, supporting himself on the shoulders of the two grand nieces.

When Nathuram Godse Fired His Shots:

Where Gandhi ji was approaching the rostrum People stood with folded hands and Gandhiji reciprocated. They made way for him to go to the rostrum, about 25 feet from the steps, where he would sit on a one-foot-high wooden dais. Nathuram Godse who was among that crowed he bowed down as he was going to touching the feet of Gandhi ji and picked his revolver from under his shirt and *Godse* shots in quick succession from close range resulting in the Mahatma's instantaneous death. He fell behind bleeding profusely and in that melee, his spectacles and footwear were thrown asunder.

Gandhiji's always using words that, "if he had to die, no precaution could save him, came true".

Gandhi never uttered 'Hey Ram' when he was shot at:

It is widely stated in book and newspaper that Gandhiji invoked God saying, "Hey Ram" as he was assassinated. There was no possibility at all of his uttering a single syllable. Though I must say, during his life time Gandhi was always used to say "I would like to die with the name of God on his lips".

In his last few days in his post-prayer speeches, Gandhiji had been repeatedly expressing the wish that God take him away since he did not want to be a silent witness to the monstrous barbarities that were going on in the country. I thought God had answered his prayer through the assassin. He had a glorious death while he was walking towards God's prayer and not on sick bed.

❍ ❍ ❍

Chapter-19

United Nations (UN) International Day of Non-Violence

Gandhi, who helped lead India to independence, has been the inspiration for non-violent movements for civil rights and social change across the world. Throughout his life, Gandhi remained committed to his belief in non-violence even under oppressive conditions and in the face of seemingly insurmountable challenges.

The theory behind his actions, which included encouraging massive civil disobedience to British law as with the historic Salt March of 1930, was that "just means lead to just ends"; that is, it is irrational to try to use violence to achieve a peaceful society. He believed that Indians must not use violence or hatred in their fight for freedom from colonialism.

Definition of Non-Violence:

The principle of non-violence - also known as non-violent resistance - rejects the use of physical violence in order to achieve social or political change.

Professor Gene Sharp, a leading scholar on non-violent resistance, used the following definition in his publication, The Politics of Nonviolent Action.- "Nonviolent action is a technique by which people who reject passivity and submission, and who see struggle as essential, can wage their conflict without violence. Nonviolent action is not an attempt to avoid or ignore conflict. It is one response to the problem of how to act effectively in politics, especially how to wield powers effectively."

There are three main categories of non-violence action:

- protest and persuasion, including marches and vigils;
- non-cooperation; and
- Non-violent intervention, such as blockades and occupations.

According to Dr. Martin Luther King Jr.-"Nonviolence means avoiding not only external physical violence but also internal violence of spirit. You not only refuse to shoot a man, but you refuse to hate him."

Non-violence is both a principle and a practice. The principle of nonviolence affirms the active use of non-coercive and non-aggressive means to create a more peaceful context. It is based on the assumption that justice will eventually prevail, that choices should be made from a place of love rather than hate, that the hurtful action, not the person, should be subdued and that voluntary suffering has value as an important facet of life.

In practice, nonviolence involves actively peaceful behaviour in the midst of conflict, becoming an example of consideration to those around us and breaking the destructive cycle of retaliation when we believe we have been wronged. It also means awareness of our own inner violence, and eliminating its negative effects upon our own intentions. Applying these principles of non-violence can reduce conflict, anger and violence on personal, local, national and global levels.

Nonviolence has come to be recognized as a powerful strategy for students, communities, disenfranchised groups and whole societies in addressing and transforming conditions.

Background of UN International day:

In January 2004, Shirin Ebadi, an Iranian political activist, lawyer, a former judge and first Muslim women Noble Peace Prize winner, had taken a proposal for an International Day of Non-Violence. The idea gradually attracted the interest of some leaders of India's Congress Party. Until a Satyagraha Conference resolution in New Delhi in January 2007, initiated by Indian National Congress President and Chairperson of the United Progressive Alliance Sonia Gandhi, and Archbishop Desmond Tutu, called upon the United Nations to adopt the idea.

Introducing the resolution in the General Assembly on behalf of 140 co-sponsors, India's Minister of state for Foreign Affairs stated that the wide and diverse sponsorship of the resolution was a reflection of the universal respect for Mahatma Gandhi and of the enduring relevance of his philosophy. Minister quoted the words of Mahatma Gandhi, "Non- violence is the greatest force at the disposal of mankind. It is mightier than the mightiest weapon of destruction devised by the ingenuity of man".

On 15 June 2007 the United Nations General Assembly voted to establish 2 October as the International Day of Non-Violence. The resolution by the General Assembly asks all members of the UN system to commemorate 2 October in "an appropriate manner and disseminate the message of non-violence, including through education and public awareness."

According to United Nations general assembly resolution A/RES/61/271 of 15 June 2007, The UN General Assembly came up to establish the International Day of Non-Violence. The day aimed to spread the message of non-violence, including through education and public awareness, around the world. The resolution reflected universal respect for Gandhi and his philosophy. October 2, which is Gandhi's birthday, was allocated as the day's date. The first International Day of Non-Violence was on October 2, 2007.

The UN recognizes a philosophical connection between the human rights principles in its universal declaration and those that Mahatma Gandhi used. He is remembered today for his contributions towards India's freedom and for sharing with the world a doctrine for dealing with injustice and disharmony. He taught people the philosophy of Ahimsa, which encourages the use of non-violence as a tool for the peaceful resolution of differences.

The resolution reaffirms "the universal relevance of the principal of non-violence".

The United Nations' (UN) International Day of Non-Violence is a global observance that promotes non-violence through education and public awareness. It is annually held on October 2 to coincide with renowned Indian leader Mahatma Gandhi's birthday. The International Day of Non-violence promotes ways to stop violence.

How UN International day is being celebrated:

Many people, governments, and non-government organizations around the world observe the International Day of Non-Violence through various events and activities such as:

- News articles and broadcast announcements promoting the day.
- Public lectures, seminars, discussions, and press conferences about non-violence.
- Photo exhibitions highlighting issues, such as the dangers of the illicit trade of small arms.
- Street awareness campaigns.
- Light ceremonies promoting non-violence and peace.
- Multi-faith prayer meetings.

Public Life on the day:

United Nations (UN) International Day of Non-Violence is a global observance but not as a public holiday.

❍❍❍

Chapter 20

Mahatma Gandhi in Nepal

Mahatma Gandhi physically never visited, but his thoughts & values were present here since a long time here in Nepal. Ancient rulers, as well as the people of Nepal were very well aware about Gandhi's movements and rendered services to the society of India, England & South Africa.

For example; A humble person of Newar community of Kathmandu, Tulsi Mehar was influenced by the ideology of 'Arya samaj'. Reading the book of Maharshi Dayanand "The light of truth." He brought himself change in his life. His vision towards social reform & development was to emphasize on women empowerment for which he was propagating about the need of education. Because of Tulsi Mehar's such actitvites late Rana Prime Minister Chandra Shamsher Jung Bahadur Rana charged him as an anti-national and decided to charge him penalty sum of two years prison and lifelong exile from the country. Hearing the decision the Tulsi Mehar stood up and humbly requested to Chandra Shamsher to forgive the punishment, because economically he was not able to pay the penalty and choose to leave the country where he could learn some skills. On the request of Tulsi Mehar Chandra shamsher decided to forgive the punishment and ordered to send him to Gandhi's Ashram at Sawarmati with Rs.100 to lean some skills. Before leaving the country Tulsi Mehar paid a last courtesy visit to Chandra shamsher. During meeting

Candra shamsher warned again to Tulsi Mehar, not to evolve in politics there, try to learn skills only. He also instructed, If needed write to me directly. That story proved that ancient rulers of Nepal were influenced by values & the social services of Mahatma Gandhi.

Tulsi Mehar was exiled in India:

Tulsi Mehar did not go Sawarmati directly. He went to Gandhi Ashram at Madras, south India. The climate, fooding, living patter, clothing, and language did not suit to Tulsi Mehar there. According to advice of fellowmen of Ashram he decided to learn skills in North India. But he was confused where to go in North India to fulfil his desire. Finally he decided to go Sawarmati, Ahmadabad, Gujrat. First time Tulsi Mehar saw Gandhi ji in a program but could not get introduces himself there. Looking towards Gandhiji he became highly impressed with his personality and he went to Sawarmati directly from there.

Tulsi Mehar with Mahatma Gandhi:

Tulsi Mehar spent nearly five years in India with Mahatma Gandhi. He lived in close association with Gandhi. He was allowed to live in the same house where Gandhiji lived. During his stay with Gandhiji he adopted Gandhi's philosophy & habit of simplicity, truthfulness and hard work. He learned several skills of arts and crafts including spinning wheels and weaving khadi. Tulsi Mehar stood himself as an honest, hard-working, peace loving and great reformist from the Gandhi Ashram. During exile period Tulsi Mehar fully utilized his time in learning.

Later Tulsi Mehar decided to serve the nation creating awareness among unprivileged Nepalese people and teaching domestic skills to uplift their economic condition. He expressed his desire to Gandhi for coming back to Nepal for above purpose. Gandhiji praised his though and allowed to go back Nepal. Gandhiji blessed him & provided two bundle of cotton, Charkha, tana & Rs. 800 cash to work in Nepal.

Having the blessings of Gandhiji came to Raxaul, India-Nepal boarder town, but he was stopped at Birgunj check post to enter in Nepal. When Gandhiji heard such news he wrote to Chandra Shamsher and requested to allow him to enter and work for social welfare in Nepal. Side by side Tulsi Mehar also wrote an application to ruler Chandra Shamsher for granting permission to enter in Nepal rendering of services for social welfare. Then he was allowed to enter in Nepal without paying custom duty of the goods which was carried from India. But Chandra Shamsher did not allow him to propagate Charkha in Nepal.

Tulsi Mehar in Nepal:

After returning Nepal Tulsi Mehar fully involved himself in Charkha movement. He wanted to help disadvantaged, poor, divorced, lower caste women of remote areas through the spinning wheel and khadi weaving. He devoted himself to promoting, encouraging and educating to disadvantaged people, to make them self -dependent. He faced many difficulties in enhancing his project. Because Rana ruler was not satisfied that he is doing only social services except politics. His project did not run smoothly due to obstruction of rulers but he was determined to achieve his aim. During that period he was arrested many times and charkhas were seized / stolen but he never gave up. But Tulsi Mehar did not lose his confidence and carried on his social work honestly without political activities against Ranas. His hard work for the society impressed Chandra Shamsher.

Establishment of "Shree Chandra Kamdhenu Charkhapracharak Mahaguthi"

The benevolent social reformer Tulsi Mehar was inspired by the value and importance of non-violence, self-reliance and truth. On his request Chandra Shamsher announces to establish "Shree ChandraKamdhenu Charkhapracharak Mahaguthi" on 1st Baishakh 1983 BS (1925 AD). It was the first social organization in Nepal, established to protect and uplift untouchables, helpless, neglected and distressed people in general and destitute women in particular followed by Gandhian philosophy. After establishment of that institution he started his work with full swing. After that he exhibited skills of cotton forming, production of thread from Charkha, teaching weaving skills at different cities of Nepal like Pokhra, Palpa, Birgunj, Biratnagar, Bhairahwa, Banepa, Bhaktapur and Kathmandu valley too. During exhibition he also gave small training for manufacturing cloths and its marketing. In the mean time, during morning & evening pray at Ashram, he started preaching about Gandhi philosophy, discipline, self- reliance, self-dependence in the society. He also started awareness program against untouchebility, social evils, and colour and cast discrimination etc. He also started "Mutthidan" (Fist Donation) to run the program. Mutthidan became popular in the society. Above program get continued in the period of Chandra Shamsher but after his death on 25 Nov.1929 that program stopped during period of Bhim Shamsher. In 1930, he was charged in anti-national activities and sent him prison. The contribution of Tulsi Mehar to the society named him "Gandhi of Nepal"

After death of Bheem Shamsher in 1923, Juddha shamsher had become Prime Minister. In that time Tulsi Meahar again got the permission to promote Charkha program.

Women empowerment:

Tulsi Meher took first step towards women's education in Nepal. Only few women were educated during that period. Realising the fact about the condition of women it was necessary to empower women for the development of the nation. So Tulsi Mehar, in 2004 BS, sent eight Nepalese women to educate them at "Kasturab Ashram" (Kasturba is the name of Gandhi's wife) of Bihar province of India. Their names are Dr. Sashi maya, Ram Pyari Mulmi, Vishnu Maya Tamote, Krishna Maya, Meera Devi Paudiyal, Debu Maya Chetri, Asta Maya, Suk Maya Lama. These Nepalese women had got their education under Gandhian environment.

Analysing the success in 2005, Tulsi Mehar encouraged and sent Bhadra Kumari Ghale, Urmila Garg, Silu singh, Mahalaxmi Shrestha, Ramvadan Joshi, Bhuneshwari satyal, Nani Hira Kansakar, Madhukari Shrestha, Kalawati Tuladhar, Angoowala Shrestha, Krishna Pyari Shrestha, Anjuwala Shrestha, Keshari Manandhar, Dr. Vimla Shrestha, Sarmistha Shrestha, Laxmi Bajracharya, 16 women, to get education at 'Mahila Vidyalaya' at Vardha Ashram, Maharastra.

After that he sent many times Nepalese women to Ashrams, Vidyalays & Mahavidyalays of Rajasthan, Bihar, U.P., Maharastra to get trainings & higher education under Gandhian culture. After coming back to Nepal those women served the nation on different levels.

Nepal Gandhi smarak Nidhi:

After the establishment of democracy in Nepal, he also established "Gandhi SmarakNidhi". In 1951 A.D King of Nepal Shree 5 Tribhuwan Bir Bikram Shah Dev and Indian Prime Minister JawaharLal Nehru inaugurated this new organization at lagan Khel, lalitpur. But it was officially registered in 2022 BS in District Administration office, Patan.

But this institution was merged in "Shree ChandraKamdhenu Charkhapracharak Mahaguthi" in 2029 BS and renamed as ***"Nepal Charkha Pracharak Gandhi Smarak MahaGuthi"***.

The organization has been regularly running the program from 1926 A.D. Thousands of Nepalese women have received different types of life skill trainings through ***Mahaguthi*** without discrimination of caste & creed, class, race, political, religious and other factors.

Gandhi Adharsa MahilaVidyalaya:

In 1953, King Tribhuwan gifted land to this organization in Manohara Kathmandu. Then he established women's school named "Gandhi Adharsa MahilaVidyalaya" the same year. With support from Indian government, industrial building was established in 1966 which was inaugurated by Indian Prime Minister Indira Gandhi. He regularly promoted this project to encourage women and children.

Gandhi- Tulsi Manohara Community Hospital:

This institution is also functioning with the help of local community on affordable cost to the poor and local people.

Mahaguthi shops:

The spinning wheel that is integral symbols associated with the Mahatma Gandhi, had changed the vision of Tulsi Mehar and he set up a retail outlet in the Mangal Bazar through where production, raw material collection and distribution was channeled. This small outlet later developed as "Mahaguthi, Craft centre in 1984.

Mahaguthi is famous centre dealing with handicraft items and commodities products at Kopundole, Laitpur. The spinning wheel has created one of Nepal's best known handicraft centres, thronged by foreign tourists for its exquisite pottery, textiles and metal etc

Tulsi Mehar Mahila Ashram:

In 1977, the Indian government bestowed the Nehru Award on Shrestha in recognition of his social service. That award money was used to found the ashram near Tribhuwan International Airport, Kathmandu. Gandhi of Nepal (Tulsi Mehar) died on Sep 27, 1978; shortly after his death the ashram was inaugurated. Ashram offers training courses in weaving, sewing, knitting and literacy classes to destitute women as well as education to their children.

Other Institutions of outside valley:

1. Gandhi Tulsi smarak Bhawan, Janakpur Dham.
2. Gandhi Tulsi Ashram, Basahiya, Dhanusa.
3. Gandhi Tulsi Gramin Dham, Mahendranagar, Dhanusa,
4. Gandhi Tulsi Dham, Amardah, Morang.

Mahatma Gandhi Scholarship:

Embassy of India provides government scholar to Nepalese students enrolled in class 11 in Nepal.

Literary works on Mahatma Gandhi in Nepal

1. Krishna Prasad Bhattarai(Late Former Prime Minister), Mahatma Gandhi sang mero teen patak ko bhet, Yugvandi, year one, issue 3, Magh 2004
2. Shushil Koirala(Late Former Prime Minister) Bapu (Nepali), Yugavandi Gandhi issue, year one, issue 3, Magh 2004BS.
3. Jeevan Chandra Koirala, Editor, Tulsi Mehar smiriti Granth (Nepali), Nepal Charkha Prachrak Gandhi-Tulsi smarak Mahaguthi-2061BS
4. Madhusudan Upadhyay, kaam Gardagardai bhetna aaye pachi ke garne (Time management of Gandhi); Time Management, 1st edition-2010, 2nd edition-2017 page-26.
5. Dr. Jagdeesh Chandra Regmi, Editor & translator, Mahatma Gandhi ka vichar haru (Nepali), Madhuwan Prakashan-Kathmandu-2075
6. Miss Bhadra Kumari Ghale(Living pupil of Gandhi),

Gandhi (Poetry in Hindi)

7. Madhav Pd. Dhimire (National Poet), Mahatma Gandhi ko Samjhana (Nepali) 2005BS.
8. Lekhnath Paudel (Kavishiromani), Amar-Jyoti ko Satya- Smiriti (Bilingual), mahamana Malaviya Mission-Nepal- January, 2019.
9. Mr. Madusudan Pandeya, an author, Edited & translated fallowing books in Nepali language on Gandhi :

• Mahatma Gandhi ka Naitik siddhant	-	Edited
• Gandhi ka Mahan Vandi	-	,,
• Gandhi vad sar sngrah	-	,,
• Gandhi Hatya Bayan sangrah	-	,,
• Janta ka Prashna Gandhi ka uttar	-	,,
• Gandhi ko Jivani	-	Translation
• Gandhi ko Hatya kin	-	,,
• Gandhi ko atma katha	-	,,
• Gandhi hatya ra ma	-	,,
• Mero sapna ko Bharat	-	,,
• Gandhi ra unka shishya	-	,,

In short

Mahatma Gandhi's dream lives on in Nepal too

❍ ❍ ❍

Bibliography

Books:

Gandhi,Mohandas karamchand; The story of my experiment with truth (An Autobiography) , Om books Internation-2018

Mukharji, Ashok & Vijay Mehta, Mahesh Sharma , Harman Singh & Arun Sharma; Mahatma Gandhi in London, High Commission of India London-2010

Gora,Lavanam & Lindley, mark; Gandhi as we have known him, National Gandhi Musiam-New Delhi 2007

Naresh; Sufism in India, National trust of India-2017

Gandhi, M. K. 1949, *Communal Unity*, Ahemdabad: Navjeevan.

Voice of Truth; Collected works of Mahata Gandhi, Volume-5

'Libya says uncatchable Belmokhtar killed', *Times of India,* (2015) 16. 6. 2015, Delhi.

Collected Works of Mahatma Gandhi (1958-83) Hundred Volumes. New Delhi: Publications Division, Ministry of Information and Broadcasting, Government of India.

Gandhi MK (1927-1929) Story of My Experiments With Truth, Vol. I (Tr. By Mahadev Desai from Gujarati) and Vo1. II Tr. (By Mahadev Desai and Pyarelal Nair (sic) from Gujarati) Ahmedabad: Navajivan Press.

Gandhi MK (1931) Hind Swaraj, or Indian Home Rule. Navajivan Press, Ahmedabad.

Gandhi MK (1930) Ethical Religion: Neethi Dharma, Tr. by A. Rama Iyer from Hindi (Madras: S. Ganesan).

Gandhi MK (1972) Satyagraha in South Africa. Navajivan, Ahmedabad.

Gandhi MK (1945) Constructive Programme: Its Meaning and Place. Navajivan, Ahmedabad.

Gandhi MK (1998) The Bhagvadgita. Orient Paperbacks, Delhi.